S0-CFN-328

# Complete EnglishSmart

## Revised and Updated!

Grammar

Comprehension

Vocabulary

Writing

Usage

Grade 1

---

ISBN: 978-1-897457-01-6

# Complete EnglishSmart Contents

ISBN: 978-1-897457-01-6

ISBN: 978-1-897457-01-6

ISBN: 978-1-897457-01-6

ISBN: 978-1-897457-01-6

# Tom's Toy Train

Tom was reading a big blue book. The book was about a toy train. The train came to life. It chugged along and took Tom around the world.

**A. Read the story and answer the questions.**

1. What colour was the book?

   BLUE

2. What was the book about?

   TOY TRAIN

3. What came to life?

   TRAIN

4. Where did Tom go?

   Around the world

ISBN: 978-1-897457-01-6

**Phonics: B and T**

**B.** 🖉 **Print B and b on the lines below.**

B

b

**C.** ✏️ **Colour the pictures that begin with the Bb sound.**

**D.** 🖉 **Print T and t on the lines below.**

T

t

**E.** ✏️ **Colour the pictures that begin with the Tt sound.**

ISBN: 978-1-897457-01-6

**Sequencing**

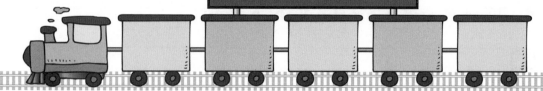

## The Toy Train

Ted has a toy train.  He takes it out of the box. He puts it together.  He flips the switch.  It goes around the track.

**F.** **Read the story and the five sentences below.  Rewrite them on the lines in the correct order.**

It goes around the track.

He puts it together.

Ted has a toy train.

He takes it out of the box.

He flips the switch.

1. _____

2. _____

3. _____

4. _____

5. _____

ISBN: 978-1-897457-01-6

## Following Directions

### G. Colour and draw.

1. Draw two toys.
2. Colour the toys.
3. Name the toys.

## Nouns (1)

- *Some nouns name people.*

### H. Underline the nouns that name people.

1. The boy is looking at the train.

2. The story is about a fireman.

3. An animal doctor helps sick animals.

4. A baker makes cookies and cakes.

ISBN: 978-1-897457-01-6

School is starting soon. Today, my mom and I are going to shop for new clothes for school. I want to buy new socks, slacks, and shoes. As a treat, maybe we will have lunch at a restaurant. Shopping for school is fun.

# ShoppingFun

**A. Answer the questions.**

1. What is starting soon?

   SCHOOL

2. When are they going to shop?

   TODAY

3. What are they shopping for?

   SOCKS SLEKS SHOES

4. What is the treat?

   RESTAURANT

ISBN: 978-1-897457-01-6

## Phonics: C and S

**B.** 🖊 **Print C and c on the lines below.**

C

c

**C.** 🖊 **Print the letter C under each picture that begins with the Cc sound.**

**D.** 🖊 **Print S and s on the lines below.**

S

s

**E.** 🖍 **Colour the pictures that begin with the Ss sound.**

ISBN: 978-1-897457-01-6

**Sequencing**

**F.  Look at the pictures.  Rewrite the sentences in the correct order.**

# Baking a Cake

We mix the ingredients.
We put the cake in the oven.
We buy the ingredients.
We spread the icing.  Yum!  Yum!

1. _____

2. _____

3. _____

4. _____

ISBN: 978-1-897457-01-6

# Nouns (2)

- *Some nouns name places.*

## G. Underline the nouns that name places.

1. The whales live in the ocean.

2. Last summer, we went to the zoo.

3. We will go to the store after lunch.

4. The park has swings.

5. We visited a farm on our vacation.

6. Let's go shopping in the new mall.

## Following Directions

## H. Colour and draw.

1. Draw a big pumpkin.
2. Colour the pumpkin orange.
3. Draw yourself in your favourite Halloween costume beside the pumpkin.

ISBN: 978-1-897457-01-6

# Muffy the New Dog

We have a new dog. His name is Muffy. He has a fluffy grey coat. He likes to play fetch. He sleeps on a carpet beside my bed. I love my new pet.

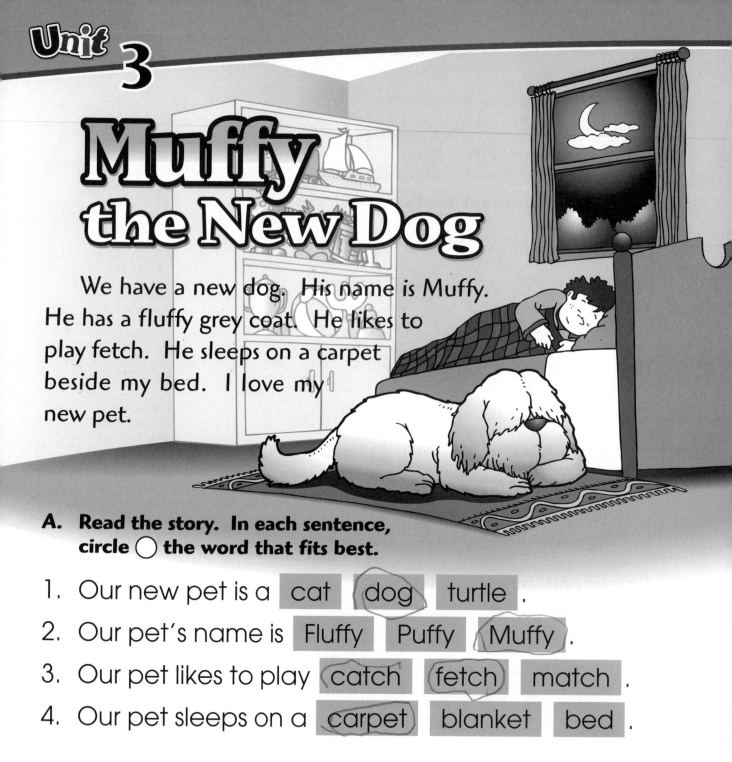

**A.** **Read the story. In each sentence, circle ◯ the word that fits best.**

1. Our new pet is a    cat    (dog)    turtle .
2. Our pet's name is    Fluffy    Puffy    (Muffy) .
3. Our pet likes to play    catch    (fetch)    match .
4. Our pet sleeps on a    (carpet)    blanket    bed .

 **Phonics: D and M**

**B.** 🖊 **Print D and d on the lines below.**

D

d

ISBN: 978-1-897457-01-6

**C.** 🖊 **Print M and m on the lines below.**

M

m

**D. Circle ◯ the correct beginning sound for each picture.**

| | | |
|---|---|---|
| **1**  d ⟨m⟩ | **2** 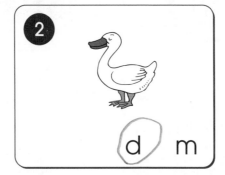 d m | **3** 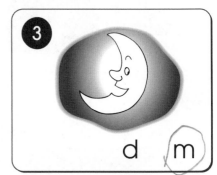 d ⟨m⟩ |
| **4** 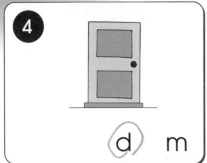 ⟨d⟩ m | **5** 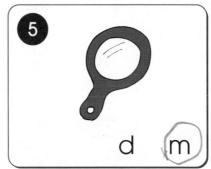 d ⟨m⟩ | **6**  ⟨d⟩ m |
| **7**  ⟨d⟩ m | **8**  d ⟨m⟩ | **9** 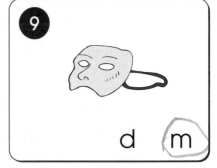 d ⟨m⟩ |
| **10**  ⟨d⟩ m | **11**  d ⟨m⟩ | **12**  ⟨d⟩ m |

ISBN: 978-1-897457-01-6

**Sequencing**

**E.  Look at the pictures.  Rewrite the sentences in the correct order.**

## Moving Day

The movers carried everything onto the truck.

The moving truck came to our house.

The house is empty.  Goodbye, house!

The moving truck drove away.

1. _____

2. _____

3. _____

4. _____

ISBN: 978-1-897457-01-6

## Nouns (3)

- Some nouns name one person or thing.  These are **Singular Nouns**.
- Some nouns name more than one person or thing.  These are **Plural Nouns**.

**F.  Circle ◯ the words that best describe the picture.**

1. boy    boys          2. girl    girls

3. bird    birds         4. dog    dogs

5. tree    trees         6. flower    flowers

7. swing    swings      8. squirrel    squirrels

ISBN: 978-1-897457-01-6

# The Race

Dan and Fiona ran a race. They started at the red line beside the fence. First, Fiona was in front. Then, Dan caught up with her. He ran past her. Finally, Fiona sped past Dan and won the race!

**A. Read the story and answer the questions.**

1. Who ran in the race?

   *dan and Fiona*

2. Where did they start?

   *red line*

3. Who was in the lead at first?

   *Fiona*

4. Who won the race?

   *Fiona*

ISBN: 978-1-897457-01-6

**Phonics: F and R**

**B.** 🖉 **Print F and f on the lines below.**

F

f

**C.** 🖍️ **Colour the objects that begin with the Ff sound.**

**D.** 🖉 **Print R and r on the lines below.**

R

r

**E. Draw three things that begin with the Rr sound.**

RAINBOW          ROAD          RUNNING

ISBN: 978-1-897457-01-6

**F.  A map helps you find your way around.  Look at the map.  Draw and colour on the map.**

1.  Draw a house <u>south</u> of the school.

2.  Colour the house red.

3.  Draw a car on the street that is <u>east</u> of the person.

4.  Draw three trees <u>north</u> of the school.

5.  Colour the leaves green and the trunks brown.

6.  Draw a swimming pool <u>west</u> of the park.

7.  Colour the swimming pool blue.

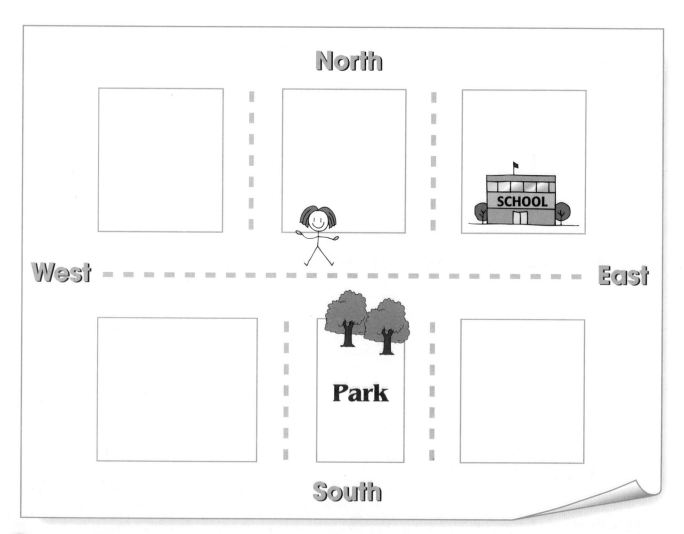

ISBN: 978-1-897457-01-6

## Nouns (4)

- Many plural nouns are formed by adding "s" to the singular nouns.
- Some are formed by adding "es".

**G. For each case, add an "s" or "es" to make more than one.**

1.   crayon + s   =

2.   box    + es =

3.   marker + s   =

4.   block  + s   =

5.   dish   + es =

6.   rug    + s   =

## Cloze

**H. The pictures tell about the missing words. Put in the words to fit the pictures.**

**1** 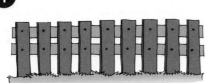  **2**   **3**

1. Roy climbed the _____ to chase the butterfly.

2. The fish swam down the _____ .

3. The _____ burned bright in the camp.

ISBN: 978-1-897457-01-6

# Plants

**A. Read the story and answer the questions.**

Plants are living things. They make their own food. They need light and water. Most plants get light from the sun and water from the rain. Light and water make plants grow.

1. What are plants?

   livingk things

2. Who makes food for plants?

   make their own

3. What two things do plants need?

   _____

4. Where do most plants get light?

   _____

5. Where do most plants get water?

   _____

ISBN 978-1-897457-01-6

## Phonics: G and P

**B.** Print G and g on the lines below.

G

g  *g g g*

**C.** Print the letter g under each picture that begins with the Gg sound.

**D.** Print P and p on the lines below.

P

p

**E.** Colour the pictures in the pizza slices that begin with the Pp sound.

ISBN: 978-1-897457-01-6

 **Sequencing**

## F.  Look at the pictures.  Rewrite the sentences in the correct order.

> We dig the soil.
> The plant sprouts.
> It rains; then the sun shines.
> We buy the seeds.
> We plant the seeds.

1. _____

2. _____

3. _____

4. _____

5. _____

ISBN: 978-1-897457-01-6

### Word Puzzles

**G.  Read the hints and write the words.**

1.  You can see it in the sky on a bright day. ☐☐☐

2.  It falls from the sky. ☐☐☐☐

3.  This is what you eat. ☐☐☐☐

4.  This is what you drink. ☐☐☐☐

5.  They are green living things that grow in the soil. ☐☐☐☐☐

### Sentences (1)

• A **Sentence** begins with a capital letter and ends with a period.

**H.  Rewrite the following as sentences.**

1.  we have a pet cat

_____

2.  the apple is tasty

_____

3.  it is sunny outside

_____

4.  there are rows and rows of corn

_____

ISBN: 978-1-897457-01-6

# Hens and Chicks

Dear Ned,

How are you? I have been learning all about chicks and hens. Did you know that chickens are birds? Hens lay eggs and sit on them to warm them. A baby chick grows inside the egg. Then the chick pecks at the shell when it is ready to hatch. Pop! A new baby chick is born.

Your friend,
Harry

## A. Read the story and answer the questions.

1. What has Harry been learning about?

_____

2. What kind of animal is a chicken?

_____

3. Where do baby chicks grow before they are hatched?

_____

4. How do baby chicks get hatched?

_____

ISBN: 978-1-897457-01-6

## Phonics: H and N

**B.** Print H and h on the lines below.

H

h

**C.** Colour the pictures that begin with the Hh sound.

**D.** Print N and n on the lines below.

N

n

**E.** Circle ◯ the correct beginning sound for each picture.

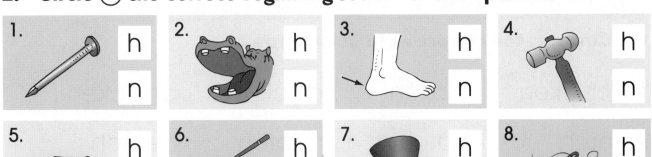

1.  h / n
2.  h / n
3.  h / n
4.  h / n
5.  h / n
6.  h / n
7.  h / n
8.  h / n

ISBN: 978-1-897457-01-6

## F. Look at the pictures. Rewrite the sentences in the correct order.

The baby chick pecks at the shell.
The chick hatches from the shell.
The hen lays an egg.
The hen sits on the egg to warm it.

1. _____

2. _____

3. _____

4. _____

## G. Circle ◯ the correct word in each row.

| | | | |
|---|---|---|---|
| 1. chicken | cicken | chickn | chiccken |
| 2. htch | hatch | haetch | heatch |
| 3. pecks | pcks | peks | peacks |

ISBN: 978-1-897457-01-6

## Sentences (2)

- A **Sentence** is a group of words. It tells a complete thought about someone or something.

  **Example:** The flower is pretty.
  (This tells something about the flower.)

**H.  Write "yes" for sentences.  Write "no" for the rest.**

1. the apple tree                              _____

2. Carrots taste good.                         _____

3. A dog barks.                                _____

4. man on the moon                             _____

5. The train chugged along.                    _____

## Following Directions

**I.   Read the sentences.  Draw and colour the Easter egg.**

1. Draw a red line near the bottom of the egg.

2. Draw five circles above the red line.  Colour them green.

3. Draw a blue line above the circles.

4. Colour the part above the blue line yellow.

5. Colour the rest of the egg your favourite colour.

ISBN: 978-1-897457-01-6

# Judy the Witch

Judy is a friendly witch.  She wears a pair of red magic jumping boots.  She likes to jump over trees and houses.  When Judy jumps, people watch.  She wishes she could jump over the moon, but her jumping boots won't go that high.

**A.  Read the story.  Circle ◯ the correct answers.**

1.  Judy is a witch.  She is _____ .

    mean          fearless          friendly

2.  Judy wears magic _____ .

    shoes          hats          boots

3.  People _____ when Judy jumps.

    wait          watch          wish

4.  Judy wishes she could jump over the _____ .

    trees          moon          houses

ISBN: 978-1-897457-01-6

**Phonics: J and W**

**B.** Print J and j on the lines below.

J

j

**C.** Colour the pictures that begin with the Jj sound.

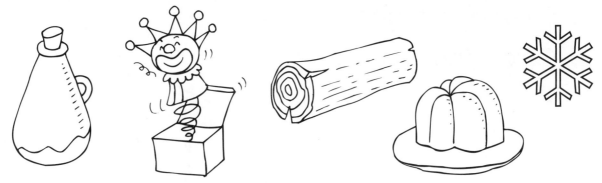

**D.** Print W and w on the lines below.

W

W

**E.** Draw the pictures that begin with the Ww sound inside the web.

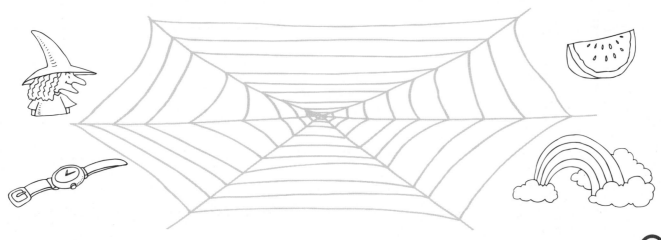

ISBN: 978-1-897457-01-6

 **Following Directions**

**F.  Read the sentences.  Follow the directions.**

1. Draw a witch in the window on the top floor.

2. Draw one door in the middle of the bottom floor.

3. Draw three jack-o'-lanterns in the windows.

4. Draw four ghosts in the garden.

5. Draw a full moon in the sky.

6. Colour the picture.

ISBN: 978-1-897457-01-6

**Verbs**

- **Verbs** are action words.

  **Example:** Mary <u>plays</u> with her dolls.

## G. Underline the verbs in these sentences.

1. Jim rides his bike.

2. David plays the guitar.

3. Kathleen looks at the stars.

4. Rob works at school.

5. Mary cooks her dinner.

6. Dad baked a cake.

7. They walked to the store.

8. The girls jumped over the rope.

9. Christina skates every week.

10. Ryan likes baseball.

ISBN: 978-1-897457-01-6

# Unit 8

## Flying Kites

Let's go fly a kite, up to the sky so bright.
Let's go fly a kite and send it soaring.

### Kites for Sale

boxes, diamonds, dragons, and more ...

### Prices start at $5.00.

**A.  Read the sign and answer the questions.**

1.  What is the sign selling?

_____

2.  What shapes are the kites?

_____

3.  What is so bright?

_____

4.  What is the starting price of the kites?

_____

5.  How many times does the word "kite(s)" appear on the sign?

_____

ISBN: 978-1-897457-01-6

**Phonics: K and V**

**B.** Print K and k on the lines below.

K

k

**C.** Join the dots beside the pictures of the words that begin with the Kk sound.

**D.** Print V and v on the lines below.

V

V

**E.** Circle ◯ the words in the word search.

vine    van    vest    violin    valentine    vase

| b | d | u | x | c | o | l | v | m | v | r | s | v | a | v | k | m | v | h |
|---|---|---|---|---|---|---|---|---|---|---|---|---|---|---|---|---|---|---|
| q | c | f | h | i | e | v | a | l | e | n | t | i | n | e | g | i | a | k |
| t | v | i | o | l | i | n | w | f | s | v | a | n | z | s | t | u | s | s |
| l | a | i | r | a | i | n | r | r | t | t | b | e | o | f | o | v | e | n |

35

ISBN: 978-1-897457-01-6

## Sequencing

**F.    Look at the pictures.  Rewrite the sentences in the correct order.**

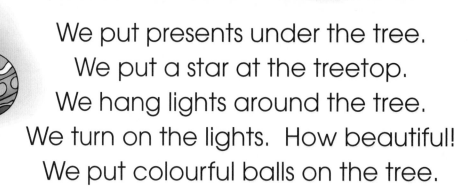

## Decorating the Christmas Tree

We put presents under the tree.
We put a star at the treetop.
We hang lights around the tree.
We turn on the lights.  How beautiful!
We put colourful balls on the tree.

1. _____

2. _____

3. _____

4. _____

5. _____

ISBN: 978-1-897457-01-6

## Sentences (3)

- A **Sentence** tells a complete thought about someone or something. It has a subject and a verb.

  **Example:** The boy jumps.

  subject ⏋  ⏌ verb

**G.  Look at the pictures.  Read the sentences.  Print the letters of the sentences in the boxes.**

A.  The pig squeals.

B.  There are three balloons.

C.  There are lots of vegetables.

D.  The goose laid a golden egg.

E.  The pizza has pepperoni on it.

F.  The mushrooms are colourful.

G.  The penguin lives in Antarctica.

H.  The goat has a kid.

I.  The bell is ringing.

ISBN: 978-1-897457-01-6

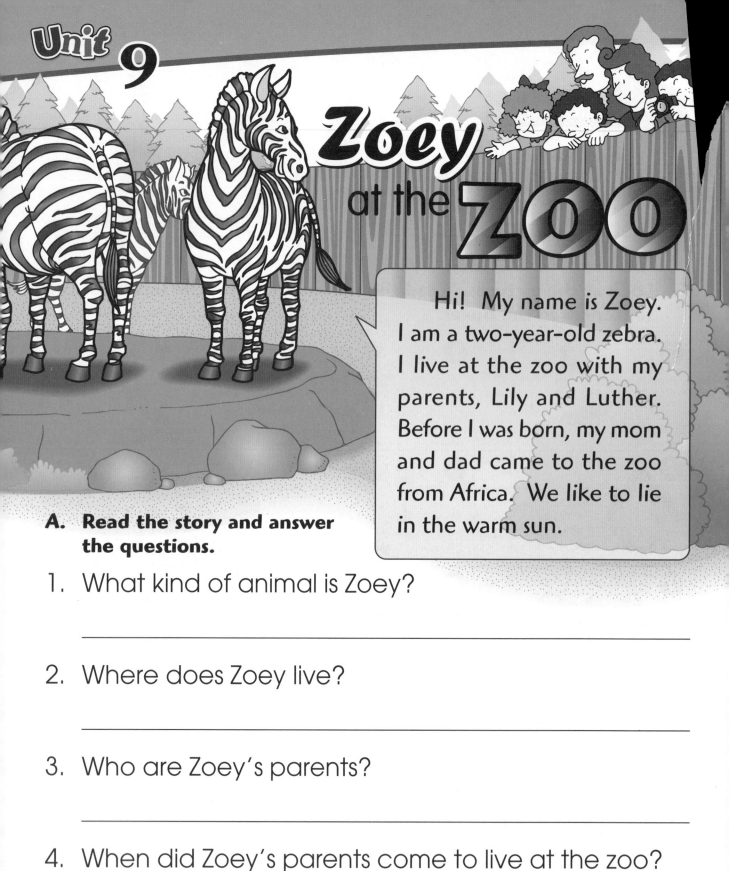

# Zoey at the ZOO

Hi! My name is Zoey. I am a two-year-old zebra. I live at the zoo with my parents, Lily and Luther. Before I was born, my mom and dad came to the zoo from Africa. We like to lie in the warm sun.

**A. Read the story and answer the questions.**

1. What kind of animal is Zoey?

   _____

2. Where does Zoey live?

   _____

3. Who are Zoey's parents?

   _____

4. When did Zoey's parents come to live at the zoo?

   _____

5. What does Zoey like to do?

   _____

ISBN: 978-1-897457-01-6

## Phonics: L and Z

**B.** Print L and l on the lines below.

L

**C.** Print Z and z on the lines below.

Z

z

**D.** Colour the pictures pink if they begin with the Ll sound.
Colour the pictures yellow if they begin with the Zz sound.

ISBN: 978-1-897457-01-6

## Unit 9

**Sequencing**

**E.** **Look at the pictures.  Rewrite the sentences in the correct order.**

Finally, I hang my picture on the wall.
First, I colour my picture.
Next, I glue my picture to the construction paper.
Then, I cut out my picture.

1. _____

2. _____

3. _____

4. _____

**Following Directions**

**F.** **Draw the following zoo animals above their names.**

| | | |
|---|---|---|
| | | |
| **a zebra** | **an elephant** | **a lion** |

ISBN: 978-1-897457-01-6

## Rhyming Words

- Words that sound the same at the end are **Rhyming Words**.

Boo!

**G. Read each word and write a word that rhymes with it.**

1. Boo! _____

2. hand _____

3. sad _____    4. seed _____

5. me _____    6. bag _____

7. money _____    8. house _____

9. tree _____    10. man _____

## Sentences (4)

- Some sentences **tell** about someone or something. They end with **Periods**.
- Some sentences **ask** about someone or something. They end with **Question Marks**.

**H. Colour** ☐T **if it is a telling sentence. Colour** ☐A **if it is an asking sentence.**

1. Have you seen the horse?    T  A

2. We have a new teacher.    T  A

3. How did he fall?    T  A

4. She went to the beach.    T  A

5. I like to play hopscotch.    T  A

41

ISBN: 978-1-897457-01-6

## Comprehension / Sequencing

**A. Read the story and write the sentences in the correct order.**

My sister and I wanted to make a tent.
First, we went to ask our mom for an old
blanket.  Then, we got some clothespins.
We took everything out to the backyard.
We hung the blanket over the clothesline.
Finally, we pinned the blanket to the line
with clothespins.  Now we are cozy inside
our tent.

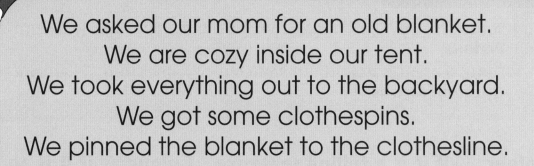

We asked our mom for an old blanket.
We are cozy inside our tent.
We took everything out to the backyard.
We got some clothespins.
We pinned the blanket to the clothesline.

1. _____

2. _____

3. _____

4. _____

5. _____

ISBN: 978-1-897457-01-6

**Phonics**

**B.   Look at each picture.  Write the beginning letter for it in the word box below it.**

1   oll

2   op

3   amp

4   un

5   all

6   at

7   ish

8   abbit

9   irl

10   ell-O

11   itch

12   izza

13   eart

14   et

15   ite

ISBN: 978-1-897457-01-6

**Following Directions**

## C. Read the sentences. Follow the directions.

1. Draw three fish in the pond.
2. Draw a house in the corner above the road.
3. Draw two children in front of the house.
4. Draw four trees near the pond.
5. Draw a car on the road.

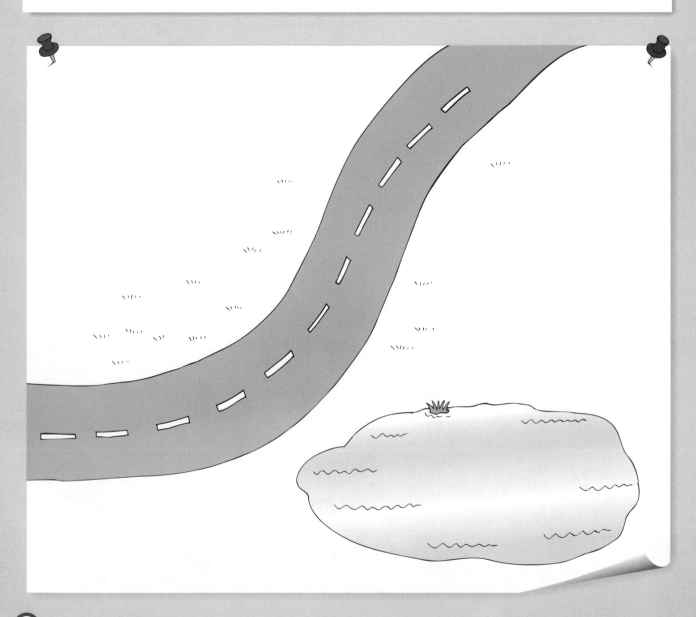

ISBN: 978-1-897457-01-6

## Word Search

**D. Circle ◯ the words in the word search.**

| train | race | blanket | light | water | hen | moon |
|---|---|---|---|---|---|---|

| witch | zoo | kite | tent | fence | boots | zebra |
|---|---|---|---|---|---|---|

| d | g | w | t | b | o | x | b | l | m | r | i | t | e | n |
|---|---|---|---|---|---|---|---|---|---|---|---|---|---|---|
| h | u | d | r | a | c | e | q | i | a | y | z | v | a | c |
| s | a | z | a | i | e | l | o | g | j | r | e | c | u | h |
| b | m | e | t | w | n | b | o | t | m | o | o | n | q | e |
| o | z | b | l | a | k | i | t | e | z | n | h | x | i | n |
| o | c | r | w | f | l | v | a | f | s | f | i | l | r | w |
| t | r | a | i | n | g | t | n | k | t | e | n | t | d | p |
| s | a | y | t | e | x | d | s | j | y | n | w | i | c | n |
| u | c | v | c | m | h | z | l | o | o | c | a | w | d | b |
| l | i | g | h | t | b | l | a | n | k | e | t | a | z | s |
| s | b | d | e | r | a | r | c | y | l | p | e | b | o | t |
| w | t | n | m | a | o | n | k | e | b | v | r | x | o | s |
| i | k | p | b | n | x | z | s | t | a | m | u | g | c | i |

ISBN: 978-1-897457-01-6

 **Nouns**

**E. Circle ◯ the word(s) to describe each picture.**

| | | |
|---|---|---|
| a bee / bees | a cup / cups | a cat / cats |

| | | |
|---|---|---|
| a sock / socks | an egg / eggs | a chick / chicks |

**F. Circle ◯ the noun that fits in each sentence.**

1. I have four   doll / dolls   .

2. The mouse ran up the   clock / clocks   .

3. The boy likes his   school / schools   .

4. The girl has a green   apple / apples   .

5. They put all the   toy / toys   in the box.

6. On the street, there are many   car / cars   .

ISBN: 978-1-897457-01-6

 **Sentences**

**G. Put each group of words in order. Rewrite it as a sentence.**

Some sentences tell about someone or something and end with periods. Some sentences ask questions and end with question marks.

1. went Pat zoo. the to

2. park. at fun They the had

3. store? Will go you the to

4. to school? How go do you

5. coming my to When you are house?

6. are rabbits There some grass. on the

1. _____

2. _____

3. _____

4. _____

5. _____

6. _____

ISBN: 978-1-897457-01-6

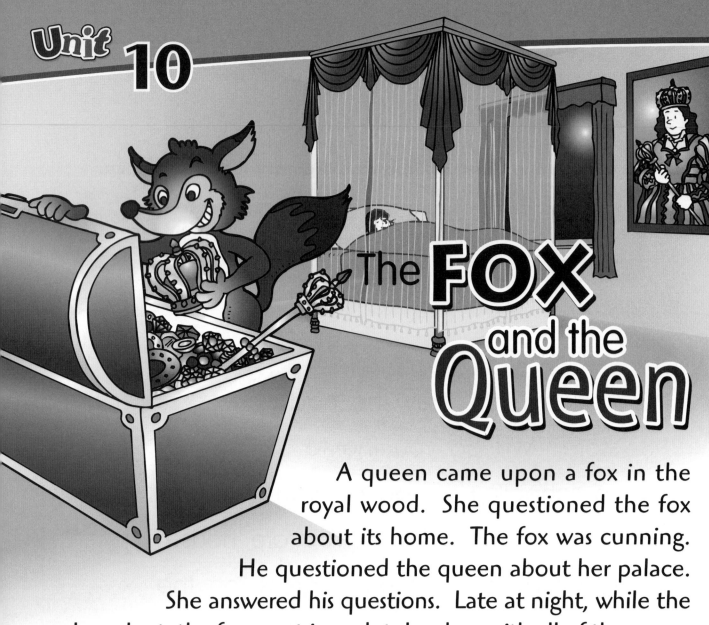

# The FOX and the Queen

A queen came upon a fox in the royal wood.  She questioned the fox about its home.  The fox was cunning.  He questioned the queen about her palace.  She answered his questions.  Late at night, while the palace slept, the fox crept in and stole a box with all of the crown jewels in it.  Poor sad queen!

## A. Fill in the blanks with words from the story.

A 1.＿＿＿＿＿＿＿ met a 2.＿＿＿＿＿＿＿ in the royal 3.＿＿＿＿＿＿＿ . The fox 4.＿＿＿＿＿＿＿ the 5.＿＿＿＿＿＿＿ about her 6.＿＿＿＿＿＿＿ . The queen answered his 7.＿＿＿＿＿＿＿ . The fox was 8.＿＿＿＿＿＿＿ . He crept into the 9.＿＿＿＿＿＿＿ . While everyone 10.＿＿＿＿＿＿＿ , he stole a 11.＿＿＿＿＿＿＿ with a lot of 12.＿＿＿＿＿＿＿ in it.

ISBN: 978-1-897457-01-6

### Phonics: Q and X

**B.** ✏️ **Print Q and q on the lines below.**

Q

q

**C.** ✏️ **Print X and x on the lines below.**

X

x

**D.** 🖍️ **Colour the pictures green if they begin with the Qq sound.**
**Colour the pictures red if they end with the Xx sound.**

ISBN: 978-1-897457-01-6

**Sequencing**

**E.** **Read the story and the instructions. Rewrite the instructions in the correct order.**

Today we made a kite. We bought sticks, paper, glue, and string. Kathleen cut the paper into a diamond shape. Next, Val cut the string. Then, Keith cut the sticks. Finally, we glued the sticks to the paper and added the string. Then we flew our kite.

**Instructions**

Fly the kite.
Buy the sticks, paper, glue, and string.
Glue the sticks and string to the paper.
Cut the paper, string, and sticks.

1. _____

2. _____

3. _____

4. _____

ISBN: 978-1-897457-01-6

 **Inflections**

**F.** **Fill in each blank with the correct word.**

1. Robert is _____ his guitar.
   play, playing

2. David and Beth are good _____ .
   dancer, dancers

3. Kathleen _____ a lot.
   talks, talking

4. Her _____ is Mary.
   name, names

5. She is _____ muffins.
   bake, baking

6. We _____ to the zoo yesterday.
   go, went

7. Where will she _____ the race?
   run, ran

8. The dog _____ at the mail carrier.
   bark, barked

ISBN: 978-1-897457-01-6

# The Wild Yak

The wild yak is a large ox. It lives in a place called Tibet. A yak can grow to be 1.8 metres tall. A wild yak has long black hair. It has long horns on its head. It eats grass.

**A. Read the story and answer the questions.**

1. What type of animal is a wild yak?

_____

2. Where does the wild yak live?

_____

3. What does the wild yak eat?

_____

4. What colour is its hair?

_____

5. How tall are some yaks?

_____

ISBN: 978-1-897457-01-6

## Phonics: Y

**B.** 🖊 **Print Y and y on the lines below.**

Y

y

**C.** Draw a line from the Y in the yo-yo to each picture that begins with the Yy sound.

ISBN: 978-1-897457-01-6

**D. Rewrite the sentences in the correct order.**

## Riding a Bike

Away you go!

Put on a helmet first.

Next, place your feet on the pedals.

Put one leg over the top of the bike to sit down.

1. _____

2. _____

3. _____

4. _____

## Question Words

- *Some sentences ask about someone or something. These are* **Questions**.
- *Some questions begin with these words:*

   **Who   What   Where   When   Why   How**

**E. Complete each question with the word that makes sense.**

1. _____ are you going?          **Who**      **Where**

2. _____ is your new teacher?     **What**     **Who**

3. _____ will you go home?        **Where**    **When**

4. _____ will you wear today?      **How**      **What**

ISBN: 978-1-897457-01-6

5. _____ did you break the toy?    **What**    **Why**

6. _____ did he get to the treetop?    **How**    **Who**

**Following Directions**

**F.  Read the sentences.  Follow the directions.**

1. Colour the spaceship your favourite colour.
2. Add a yellow happy face on Dox's T-shirt.
3. Colour Quin's T-shirt orange.
4. Draw Quox next to Quin.

Dox

Quin

ISBN: 978-1-897457-01-6

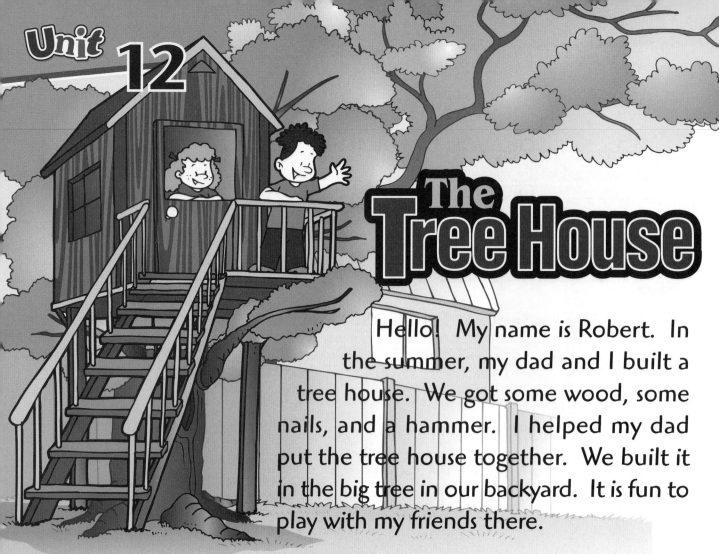

# The Tree House

Hello! My name is Robert. In the summer, my dad and I built a tree house. We got some wood, some nails, and a hammer. I helped my dad put the tree house together. We built it in the big tree in our backyard. It is fun to play with my friends there.

**A. Read the story and answer the questions.**

1. What is the name of the boy in the story?

   _____

2. What did the boy build with his father?

   _____

3. What did they use to build it?

   _____

4. Where did they build it?

   _____

5. When did they build it?

   _____

ISBN: 978-1-897457-01-6

## Phonics: a, e, i, o, and u

**B. Write "a", "e", "i", "o", or "u" in each box. Then read out the words.**

1. n ☐ t

2. c l ☐ c k

3. g ☐ f t

4. p ☐ n g u i n

5. l ☐ p s

6. l a d y b ☐ g

7. h ☐ t

8. d ☐ l l

9. ☐ m b r ☐ l l ☐

## Sequencing

**C.** **Look at the pictures.  Rewrite the sentences in the correct order.**

I let the yo-yo fall.

My yo-yo goes up and down.

I wind the string around my yo-yo.

I have a yo-yo.

1. _____

2. _____

3. _____

4. _____

## Word Order in Sentences

- Some sentences begin with capital letters and end with periods.
- Sentences make sense.

ISBN: 978-1-897457-01-6

**D. Put the words in the correct order to make sentences. Write the sentences on the lines below.**

**Example:** apple is The juicy.
The apple is juicy.

1. A long horns. wild has yak

_____

2. smile. a have You pretty

_____

3. need yellow I crayon. a

_____

4. cage. bird sings The a in

_____

5. like play to I with dog. my

_____

6. my Look dog. at cute

_____

7. are yummy bananas. They

_____

ISBN: 978-1-897457-01-6

# Bart the Bear

Bart is a black bear. He lives in Canada. Bart sleeps all winter long. When he wakes up, he is very hungry. He goes looking for plants, nuts, roots, and berries to eat. His favourite food is honey.

**A. Read the story. Circle ◯ the correct answers.**

1. The story is about a _____ .
   beaver     bear     bird

2. Bart sleeps during _____ .
   summer     day     winter

3. When Bart wakes up, he feels _____ .
   happy     cold     hungry

4. Bart likes to eat _____ .
   roots and berries     apples and oranges

5. _____ is his favourite food.
   Grass     Honey     Hay

6. Black bears live in _____ .
   Canada     Mexico     France

ISBN: 978-1-897457-01-6

**Ending Sounds: B, D, and T**

**B.** Print the letters that name the ending sounds.

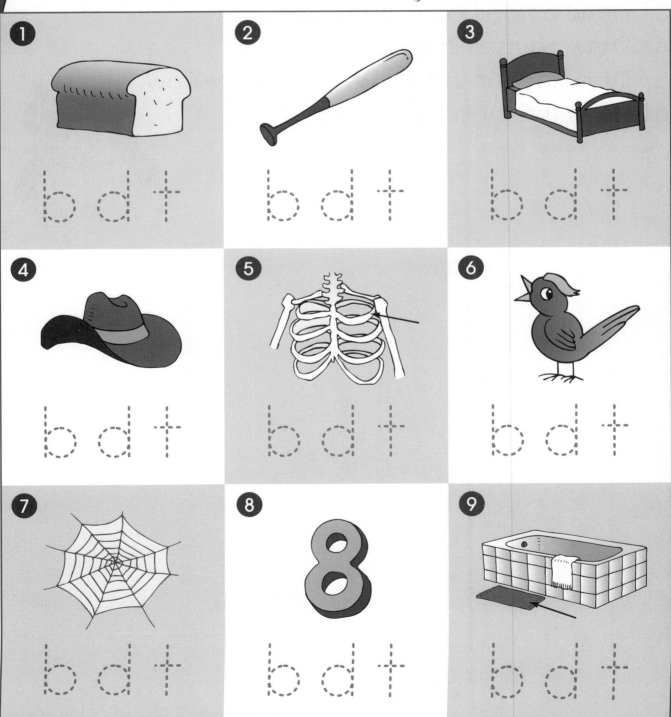

1. b d t

2. b d t

3. b d t

4. b d t

5. b d t

6. b d t

7. b d t

8. b d t

9. b d t

**Following Directions**

## C. Read the sentences. Follow the directions.

1. Draw a tree and colour the trunk brown.
2. Draw the leaves on the tree. Colour them green.
3. Draw a tree house in the tree.
4. Draw yourself in the picture.
5. Draw the sun in the sky. Colour it yellow.
6. Draw three birds in the sky.

ISBN: 978-1-897457-01-6

## Sentence Structures

**D. Put the words in the correct order to make sentences.**

1. many   bluebirds   There   are   sky.   the   in

_____

2. are   skates?   my   Where

_____

3. flowers   are   bloom.   The   in

_____

## Synonyms

• **Synonyms** are words that have the same meaning.

**E.   Circle ◯ the synonym for each word on the left.**

| 1. below | in | under | inside | out |
|----------|------|-------|--------|---------|
| 2. up | down | out | big | above |
| 3. big | over | under | large | outside |
| 4. small | tiny | big | huge | tall |

ISBN: 978-1-897457-01-6

# Making Blueberry Jam

My mom and I are going to make blueberry jam. First, we go to our secret place to pick blueberries from the bushes. Then we sit and pick all the blueberries we want. When we get home, we clean the berries and take out the leaves. Mom puts them in a pot with water and sugar and boils it on the stove. When it is cooled, we taste it. Yum! Yum!

**A. Read the instructions. Answer the questions.**

1. What is the first thing to do to make blueberry jam?

_____

2. Where do they go to pick berries?

_____

3. What do they do after they bring the berries home?

_____

ISBN: 978-1-897457-01-6

**Ending Sounds: F, M, and R**

d r u (m)

j a (r)

l e a (f)

**B.** Colour the pictures in each group that end with the sound of the letter.

f

m

r

ISBN: 978-1-897457-01-6

## Filling in Speech Bubbles

**C.** **Fill in the words that you think these characters are saying to each other.**

## Crossword Puzzle

**D.** **Read the clues and complete the crossword puzzle.**

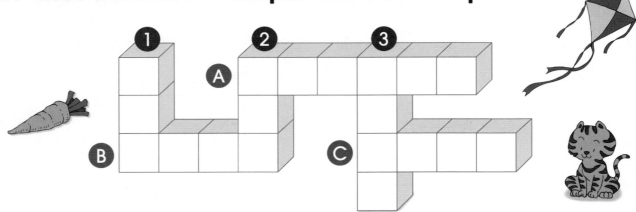

| **Across** | A. | what rabbits like to eat |
| | B. | place to sleep when camping |
| | C. | Let's fly a _____ . |

| **Down** | 1. | flying mammal that hunts at night |
| | 2. | pet that purrs |
| | 3. | used to gather cut grass |

ISBN: 978-1-897457-01-6

**Tenses**

**E.  Fill in each blank with the correct word.**

1. We _____ play, played at the park yesterday.

2. She _____ is, were the best dancer here.

3. He _____ give, gave them some gum.

4. You _____ will, did go with them tomorrow.

5. We _____ had, has a good time singing.

6. It _____ rained, rain all morning today.

7. She _____ won, win the race.

8. Little Jim _____ want, wanted to eat the candy.

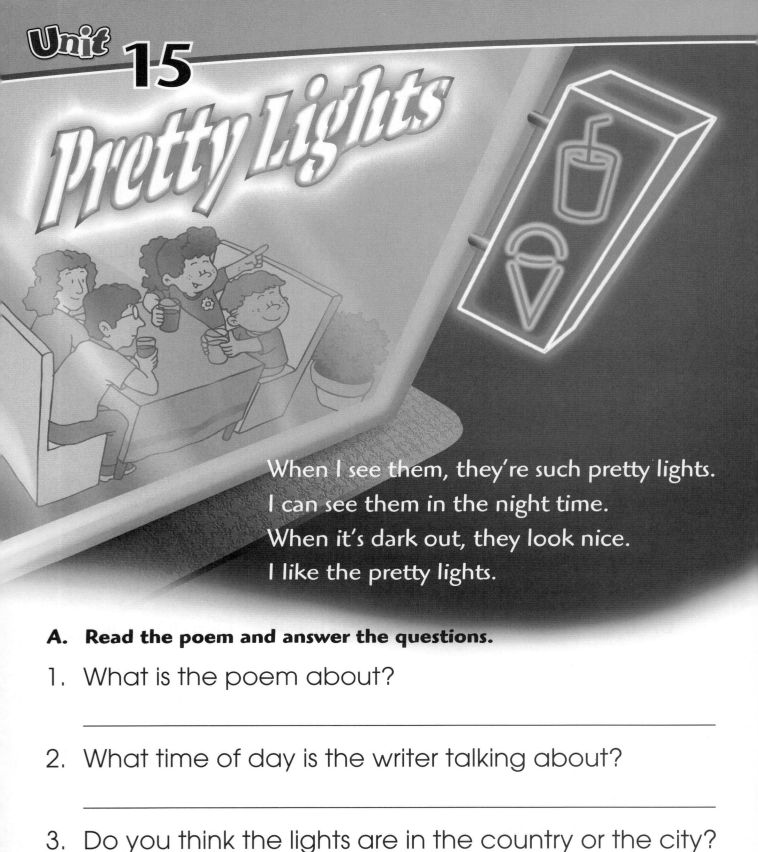

# Unit 15

## Pretty Lights

When I see them, they're such pretty lights.
I can see them in the night time.
When it's dark out, they look nice.
I like the pretty lights.

**A. Read the poem and answer the questions.**

1. What is the poem about?

   _____

2. What time of day is the writer talking about?

   _____

3. Do you think the lights are in the country or the city?

   _____

4. Do you ever see pretty lights?  Where?

   _____

ISBN: 978-1-897457-01-6

## Ending Sounds: G, K, and S

**B.** Colour the pictures in each group that end with the sound of the letter.

ju**g**

loc**k**

scissor**s**

ISBN: 978-1-897457-01-6

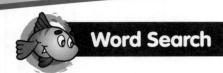 **Word Search**

**C.** Find these words in the word search. Highlight them with a yellow crayon.

| stop | children | coin | bat | turtle | leaf |
|------|----------|------|-----|--------|------|
| castle | tomorrow | light | hop | today | school |

| B | L | N | P | E | C | A | S | T | L | E | E | S |
|---|---|---|---|---|---|---|---|---|---|---|---|---|
| N | R | R | A | K | V | O | M | U | K | X | N | N |
| G | F | O | C | H | I | L | D | R | E | N | T | Y |
| J | U | X | O | M | J | D | E | T | A | U | R | B |
| S | T | M | I | R | O | T | W | L | I | G | H | T |
| U | J | F | N | E | C | H | J | E | O | C | L | V |
| B | S | J | Y | F | L | C | N | S | E | V | O | I |
| K | T | A | V | C | N | E | D | B | G | H | P | S |
| T | O | M | O | R | R | O | W | S | C | L | O | D |
| O | P | B | C | A | C | L | E | V | Y | E | G | E |
| D | R | L | H | G | O | C | A | C | B | A | T | R |
| A | U | I | V | D | J | H | F | R | A | F | S | M |
| Y | N | C | S | C | H | O | O | L | U | E | B | I |
| V | B | A | F | J | S | P | L | D | T | S | U | A |

ISBN: 978-1-897457-01-6

## Antonyms

- **Antonyms** *are words that are opposites.*
  **Examples:** hot ⟶ cold
  long ⟶ short

**D.** Circle ◯ the antonym of the first word in each row.

| | | | | |
|---|---|---|---|---|
| 1. | **day** | night | week | time |
| 2. | **hard** | rough | soft | slimy |
| 3. | **stop** | red | look | go |
| 4. | **white** | blue | green | black |
| 5. | **no** | maybe | was | yes |
| 6. | **happy** | sad | feel | fun |
| 7. | **big** | wide | little | huge |
| 8. | **asleep** | tired | night | awake |

ISBN: 978-1-897457-01-6

**A. Read the sentences in each group. Circle ⃝ the correct answer.**

1. I am round.
   I make a sound.
   You use sticks to play me.
   What am I?

   **a doll    a drum
   a guitar    a ball**

2. I am hot.
   I look yellow.
   I heat the Earth.
   What am I?

   **the sun    the star
   the sky    the moon**

3. I am round.
   I can bounce.
   I can roll.
   What am I?

   **a ball    a book
   a doll    a flower**

4. I am round.
   I am made of metal.
   You can buy things with me.
   What am I?

   **a coin    a candle
   a crane    a carrot**

5. I can be hard.
   I can be soft.
   You read me.
   What am I?

   **a book    a box
   a hook    a doll**

ISBN: 978-1-897457-01-6

## Ending Sounds: L, N, and P

b a l **l**      f a **n**      c u **p**

**B.** Draw a line from each letter to the picture that ends with the sound of that letter.

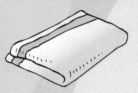

 **l**

 **n**

 **p**

ISBN: 978-1-897457-01-6

**Following Directions**

## C. Read the sentences.  Follow the directions.

1. Draw your family.
2. Draw your house.
3. Draw your favourite pet.
4. Draw your car.
5. Draw your favourite toy.
6. Write your name.

ISBN: 978-1-897457-01-6

## Rhyming Words

- Words that rhyme sound the same at the end.
  **Example:** cat    bat    sat

**D.** Circle ◯ the word in each row that rhymes with the first word.

1. **rug**      cup        mug        hot

2. **go**       to         gone       so

3. **fun**      here       run        walk

4. **tag**      game       it         bag

5. **red**      bed        stop       blue

6. **hot**      cold       pot        cat

7. **sit**      up         at         it

8. **book**     read       ton        hook

9. **cake**     eat        bake       ice

ISBN: 978-1-897457-01-6

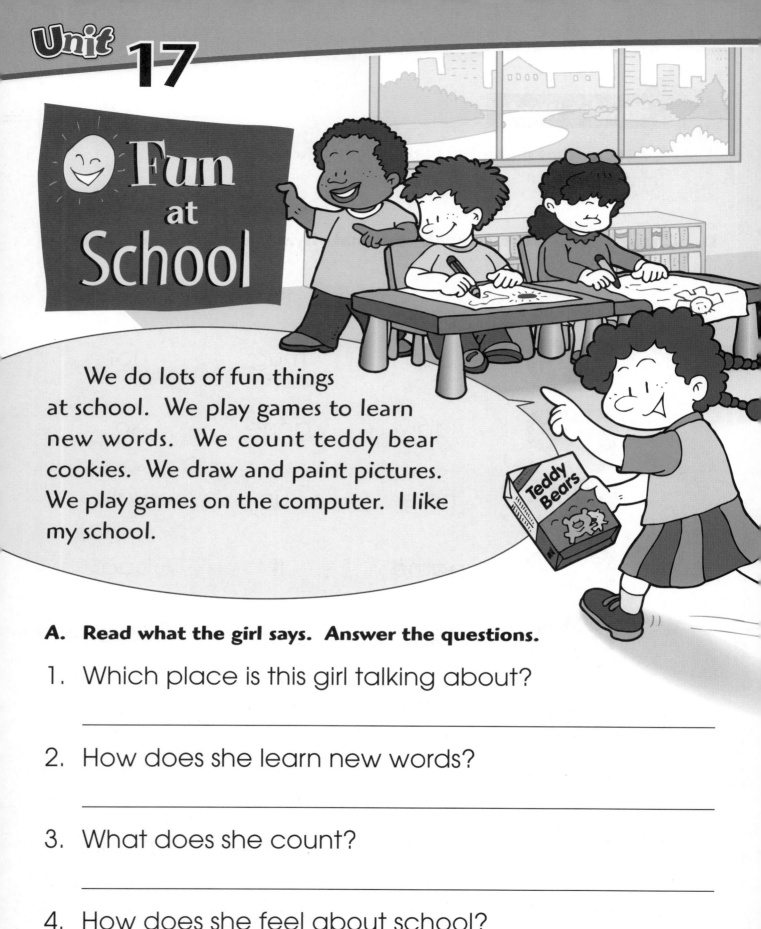

**Fun at School**

We do lots of fun things at school. We play games to learn new words. We count teddy bear cookies. We draw and paint pictures. We play games on the computer. I like my school.

**A. Read what the girl says. Answer the questions.**

1. Which place is this girl talking about?

_____

2. How does she learn new words?

_____

3. What does she count?

_____

4. How does she feel about school?

_____

ISBN: 978-1-897457-01-6

## Phonics: Beginning and Ending Sounds

**B.  Look at the pictures.  Fill in the missing letters for each word.**

1

| | u | |
|---|---|---|

2

| | a | |
|---|---|---|

3

| | e | |
|---|---|---|

4

| | o | |
|---|---|---|

5

| | a | l | |
|---|---|---|---|

6

| | e | n | |
|---|---|---|---|

7

| | a | |
|---|---|---|

8

| | a | |
|---|---|---|

9

| | i | r | |
|---|---|---|---|

10

| | o | o | |
|---|---|---|---|

11

| | a | |
|---|---|---|

12

| | a | |
|---|---|---|

ISBN: 978-1-897457-01-6

**Word Search**

**C. Find these words in the word search. Put a line through each word when you find it.**

box    ball    doll    cat    bad    bib
dog    drum    bird    pan    door    bed
cup    hat    cap    top    bag    tent

| G | A | B | F | H | B | K | S | N | O | B | M | W |
|---|---|---|---|---|---|---|---|---|---|---|---|---|
| U | T | N | G | D | O | L | L | T | N | A | C | F |
| D | B | L | H | O | X | A | B | I | R | D | C | M |
| U | E | O | T | O | U | F | C | U | P | Q | J | Q |
| V | R | F | U | R | L | P | Q | D | V | W | V | F |
| X | Y | B | H | T | C | A | P | R | J | B | A | G |
| T | N | G | D | H | U | N | Q | U | X | I | V | N |
| R | O | Y | X | A | M | P | C | M | O | B | H | B |
| S | T | E | N | T | J | Y | N | X | I | T | R | E |
| E | K | V | R | N | W | B | A | L | L | G | D | D |
| O | L | X | S | U | F | C | P | E | F | W | O | X |
| T | O | P | C | A | T | I | G | H | G | T | G | A |

ISBN: 978-1-897457-01-6

## Word Families

**D.** **Read the word at the top of each column. Print the words that are from the same word family.**

*They sound the same at the end.*

| 1. c a t | 2. c r i b | 3. s a d |
|---|---|---|
| ☐ a t | ☐ i b | ☐ a d |
| ☐ a t | ☐ i b | ☐ a d |
| ☐ a t | ☐ i b | ☐ a d |

| 4. s i t | 5. c a p | 6. l i d |
|---|---|---|
| ☐ i t | ☐ a p | ☐ i d |
| ☐ i t | ☐ a p | ☐ i d |
| ☐ i t | ☐ a p | ☐ i d |

ISBN: 978-1-897457-01-6

# Sweet Maple Syrup

One sunny morning in March, Sam went on a trip to the Sugar Bush. He saw many tall maple trees. The sap from the trees flowed into buckets. The sap was boiled in a big kettle to make thick, sweet maple syrup. Yum! Yum!

## A. Circle ◯ the correct answers.

1. Sam went to the _____ .

   maple garden          Sugar Bush          zoo

2. There were many tall _____ trees.

   pine                  maple               apple

3. The sap ran into _____ .

   pockets               baskets             buckets

4. The sap became _____ .

   syrup                 sugar               candy

ISBN: 978-1-897457-01-6

## Crossword Puzzle

**B. Read the clues and complete the crossword puzzle.**

SWEET    MAPLE
TALL    BUCKETS    THICK
MARCH    SYRUP

### Across

A. The month before April
B. The opposite of short
C. It is made from sap.

### Down

1. This taste is good.
2. Pails
3. The opposite of thin
4. A kind of tree

ISBN: 978-1-897457-01-6

# Unit 18

**Phonics: Consonant Blends**

**C.** Colour the pictures that begin with the given blends.

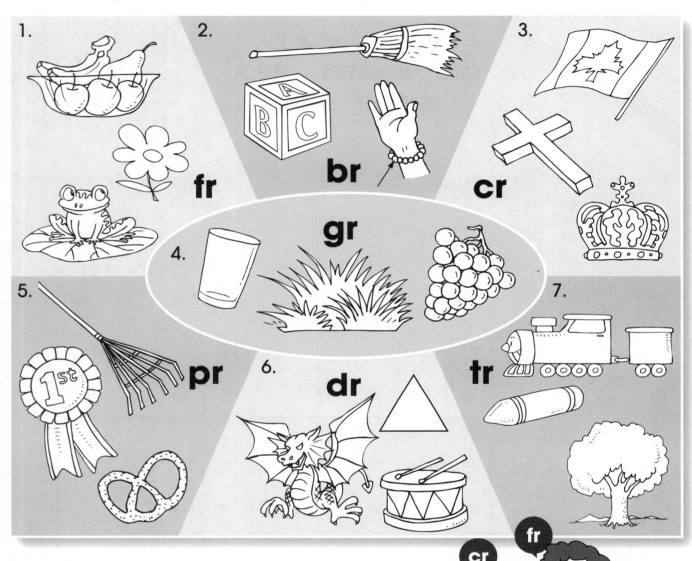

**D.** Complete each word with a correct blend from above.

1. __ __ __ oom
2. __ __ __ oss
3. __ __ apes
4. __ __ ayon
5. __ __ ass
6. __ __ um
7. __ __ og
8. __ __ ee
9. __ __ ize
10. __ __ own

ISBN: 978-1-897457-01-6

## Rhyming Words

**E. Draw lines to join the words that rhyme.**

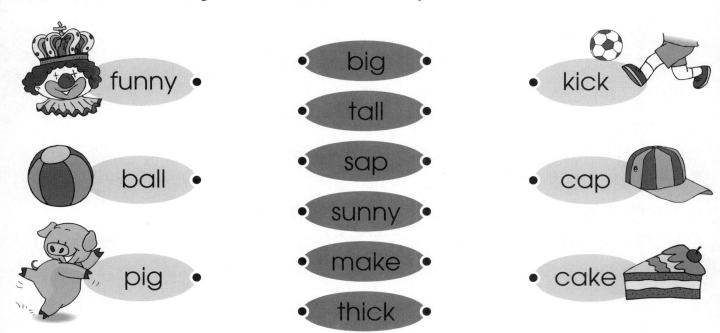

funny

ball

pig

big

tall

sap

sunny

make

thick

kick

cap

cake

## Sentences

**F. Cross out the sentence that does not belong.**

1. My name is Jenny. The children went on a trip. They saw many tall trees.

2. I have pancakes for breakfast. I put maple syrup on the pancakes. The cat is sleeping.

3. We have a maple tree in front of our house. It is tall. Go Leafs go!

4. Pat has one brother and one sister. April is in spring. December is in winter.

ISBN: 978-1-897457-01-6

**Comprehension**

**A. Read the *story* and answer the questions.**

My favourite hobby is collecting rocks. From summer to fall, I go for long walks with my mom and we stop and pick up rocks along the way on the sides of the roads and on paths. All the rocks are different. Some have spots, some have stripes, and others have many colours. Some are pink, some are blue, and some are grey or black. I have more than a hundred rocks in my collection now.

1. What is the boy's favourite hobby?

   _____

2. With whom does he go for long walks?

   _____

3. When does he collect the rocks?

   _____

4. Where do they find the rocks?

   _____

5. How do the rocks look?

   _____

6. How many rocks does he have in his collection?

   _____

ISBN: 978-1-897457-01-6

## Phonics: Short Vowels a, e, i, o, and u

**B.  Look at each picture.  Fill in the missing vowel.**

| 1 | 2 | 3 |
|---|---|---|
| c ☐ t | l ☐ ps | l ☐ g |

| 4 | 5 | 6 |
|---|---|---|
| h ☐ nd | r ☐ g | b ☐ ll |

| 7 | 8 | 9 |
|---|---|---|
| s ☐ x | d ☐ g | c ☐ p |

| 10 | 11 | 12 |
|---|---|---|
| t ☐ p | t ☐ nt | f ☐ sh |

ISBN: 978-1-897457-01-6

## Beginning and Ending Sounds

**C.** For 1 to 4, circle ◯ the beginning sounds. For 5 to 8, circle ◯ the ending sounds.

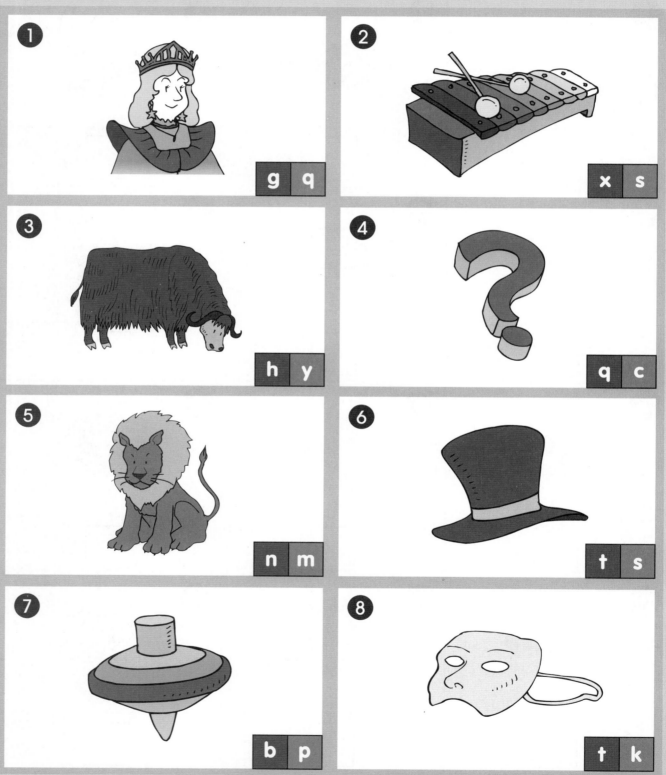

**1** | g | q

**2** | x | s

**3** | h | y

**4** | q | c

**5** | n | m

**6** | t | s

**7** | b | p

**8** | t | k

ISBN: 978-1-897457-01-6

**Match-up Meanings**

**D. Draw a line to join each word with its meaning.**

1. **hat**          something to cook in

2. **cat**          an adult human male

3. **bat**          something to wear on your head

4. **man**          made of a metal, like tin

5. **fan**          an animal with whiskers and a long tail

6. **can**          a flying mammal

7. **van**          It keeps you cool in summer.

8. **pan**          A fish has one.

9. **fin**          It carries a lot of people.

 **Riddles**

**E. Solve the riddles.**

1. What's a bridge with seven colours?

   _____

2. What rises in the east and sets in the west?

   _____

ISBN: 978-1-897457-01-6

**Sequencing**

**F.** **Read the sentences below. Put them in the correct order. Add an ending of your own in the box.**

> I like to make ice cream cones. My favourite flavour is strawberry. First, I go to the cupboard and take a cone from the package. Then, I get the ice cream from the freezer. I use a scoop to pick up the ice cream and place it on top of the cone. Finally, I put some sprinkles on top.

Take the ice cream out of the freezer.
Use a scoop to pick up the ice cream.
Put some sprinkles on top.
Go to the cupboard.
Take out a cone.

1. _____

2. _____

3. _____

4. _____

5. _____

6.

ISBN: 978-1-897457-01-6

## Synonyms and Antonyms

**G.** Colour ⭐ if the words are synonyms.
Colour ◯ if they are antonyms.

Synonyms are words that have the same meaning. Antonyms are words that are opposites.

| small    tiny | up    down | |
| :---: | :---: | :---: |
| ⭐  ◯ | ⭐  ◯ | |
| big    large | below    under | happy    sad |
| ⭐  ◯ | ⭐  ◯ | ⭐  ◯ |
| stop    go | big    little | yes    no |
| ⭐  ◯ | ⭐  ◯ | ⭐  ◯ |

## Rhyming Words

Rhyming words are those that sound the same at the end.

**H.** Circle ◯ the word that does not rhyme with others in each row.

1.  bug    duck    hug    jug    mug

2.  bake    cake    lake    made    take

3.  dough    go    no    so    to

4.  ball    fall    hall    pull    tall

5.  bunny    fully    funny    honey    sunny

ISBN: 978-1-897457-01-6

ISBN: 978-1-897457-01-6

Outside

Inside

# Nouns (1)

**Nouns**

A **noun** is a word that names a person, an animal, a place, or a thing.

*Examples*:  teacher (a person)
horse (an animal)
park (a place)
doll (a thing)

## A. Write the nouns on the correct cards.

school    mother    mitten    rabbit
moose    beach    nurse    jam

**Place**

_____

_____

**Thing**

_____

_____

**Person**

_____

_____

**Animal**

_____

_____

ISBN: 978-1-897457-01-6

**B. Look at these words. Some are nouns and some are not. Colour the nouns.**

| | | | | |
|---|---|---|---|---|
| carrot | eat | chilly | star | boat |
| table | water | write | worker | grass |
| make | dim | singer | song | bag |

**C. Circle ○ the nouns in the sentences.**

1. The boy is thirsty.

2. The girl is eating an apple.

3. The cat likes milk.

4. My dog is under the table.

5. The baby smiles.

6. The fish swims in the river.

7. The mall is close to our house.

8. The new storybook is interesting.

ISBN: 978-1-897457-01-6

## Common and Proper Nouns

A **common noun** names any person, animal, place, or thing.

*Examples*:  doctor (person)      dog (animal)
              country (place)     apple (thing)

A **proper noun** names a specific person, animal, place, or thing.  It always begins with a capital letter.

*Examples*:  Dr. Jones (person)   Dalmatian (animal)
              Canada (place)       Red Delicious (thing)

**D. Read the nouns.  Put them in the correct cheese.  Begin the proper nouns with capital letters.**

car   barbie   ottawa   school   kim   mouse

Common Noun

teacher

Proper Noun

Pug

ISBN: 978-1-897457-01-6

Days of the week, months of the year, and festivals are proper nouns. They always begin with capital letters.

*Examples*:   <u>Monday</u> is the second day of the week.
<u>Halloween</u> is in <u>October</u>.

**E.  Fill in the blanks with the correct proper nouns.  Begin them with capital letters.**

sunday    tuesday    saturday    january    december
christmas    easter    new year's day

1. The 25th of _____ is _____ .

2. The candy shop is closed on the weekend, that is
_____ and _____ .

3. The first day of _____
is _____ .

4. Children eat chocolate
eggs at _____ .

5. _____ is the
third day of the week.

> ### Singular and Plural Nouns
>
> A **singular noun** names one person, animal, place, or thing.
>
> *Examples*: girl, beaver, park, pencil
>
>  A **plural noun** names more than one person, animal, place, or thing. Many plural nouns are formed by adding "s" to the singular nouns.
>
> *Examples*: girls, beavers, parks, pencils

## A. Circle ◯ the word that describes each picture.

1.

flower / flowers

2.

owl / owls

3.

castle / castles

4.

kid / kids

ISBN: 978-1-897457-01-6

**B. Look at each picture. Draw a picture to make it plural in the box. Write the plural noun by adding "s" to the singular noun.**

1. mushroom

_____

2. bear

_____

3. balloon

_____

4. star

_____

ISBN: 978-1-897457-01-6

## Plural Nouns

Some **plural nouns** are formed by adding "es" to the singular nouns.

If a noun ends in "s", "x", "ch", or "sh", add "es" to form its plural.

*Examples*:  cross → crosses    peach → peaches

**C.  Change each singular noun to plural by adding "es".  Write the plural noun under the correct picture.**

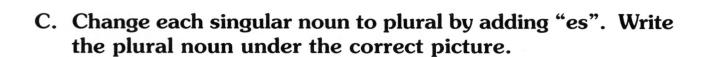

box    sandwich    glass    dish

1.

_____

2.

_____

3.

_____

4.

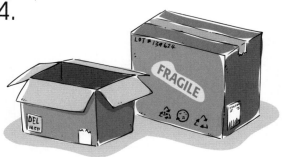

_____

ISBN: 978-1-897457-01-6

**D. Fill in the blanks with the plural form of the given nouns.**

1. The two (fox) _____ are playing happily.

2. There are so many (switch) _____ here.  Which one should I press?

3. I put my friends' (address) _____ in this book.

4. There are two cats behind the (bush) _____ .

5. How many (bench) _____ are there in this park?

**E. Circle ○ the misspelled plural form in each sentence.  Write the correct spelling on the line.**

1. There are beachs along the coast.  _____

2. They dress up as clownes and witches.

_____

3. How many brushs do the girls need?

_____

4. Octopuses have eight leges.

_____

> ### He, She, It, and They
>
> A **pronoun** is a word that replaces a noun. "**He**", "**she**", "**it**", and "**they**" are some of the pronouns.
>
> *Example*:  Colin has a new robot.
>  <u>He</u> likes it very much.
>
> In the second sentence, "he" replaces "Colin".

## A. Match the pictures with the correct pronouns. Write the letters.

| He | She | It | They |
|----|-----|-----|------|
|    |     |     |      |

ISBN: 978-1-897457-01-6

**B. Write the correct pronouns for the words.**

1. two teachers [ ]    2. Mr. Wright [ ]

3. some birds [ ]    4. a book [ ]

5. Sally [ ]    6. the actor [ ]

7. the kitten [ ]    8. Mom [ ]

**C. Fill in the blanks with the correct pronouns.**

1. The boys had a game of soccer. _____ are very tired now.

2. Audrey has a dog. _____ walks it in the park every day.

3. There is an apple on the table. _____ is big.

4. Dad bought some strawberries. _____ are bright red in colour.

5. Ken is sad. _____ has lost his favourite toy car.

6. Kara saw a tiny bird in her backyard. _____ was a hummingbird.

## I, You, and We

"**I**" is used when you are talking about yourself.
"**You**" is used when you are talking to another person.
"**We**" is used when you are talking about yourself and another person or other people.

*Examples*:  I'm going hiking this Sunday.
Will you join me?
We can set out in the morning.

---

**D. Write pronouns to replace the pictures on the lines.**

**I**  **You**  **We**

Kathy and 1.  went

hiking last week. 2.  walked by a creek. 3.

saw some ducks there. 4.  wanted to take a better

look at them, but 5.  tripped and fell into the water.

Kathy laughed. To hide my embarrassment, 6.  said,

"It's so hot today 7.  just wanted to take a cool bath

in the water. Would 8.  like to join me?"

1. _____  2. _____  3. _____  4. _____

5. _____  6. _____  7. _____  8. _____

ISBN: 978-1-897457-01-6

**E. Rewrite the sentences by replacing the underlined words with the correct pronouns.**

1. <u>Kate, Paul, and I</u> went to the beach.

   _____

2. <u>The beach</u> was a beautiful beach.

   _____

3. <u>Paul</u> built a sandcastle.

   _____

4. <u>The sandcastle</u> was as tall as Paul.

   _____

5. <u>Kate</u> found two sand dollars.

   _____

6. <u>The sand dollars</u> were light pink in colour.

   _____

7. Kate asked, "Can <u>Kate</u>
   keep the sand dollars?"

   _____

   _____

   _____

### A and An

"A" and "an" are **articles**. They come before singular nouns.
"**A**" is used before a singular noun that begins with a consonant.
"**An**" is used before a singular noun that begins with a vowel.

*Examples*:  a car    a monkey
an apple   an igloo

## A. Draw lines to match the nouns with the correct articles.

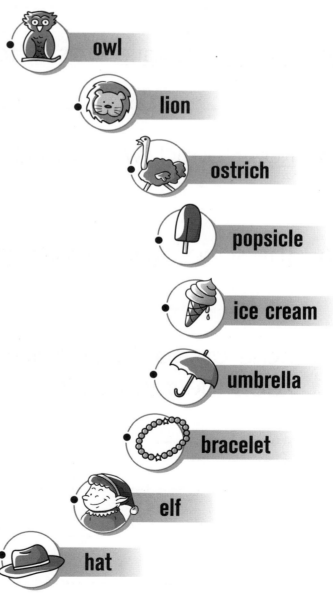

owl

lion

ostrich

popsicle

ice cream

a

an

umbrella

bracelet

elf

hat

ISBN: 978-1-897457-01-6

# B. Look at each picture. Write what it is with the correct article.

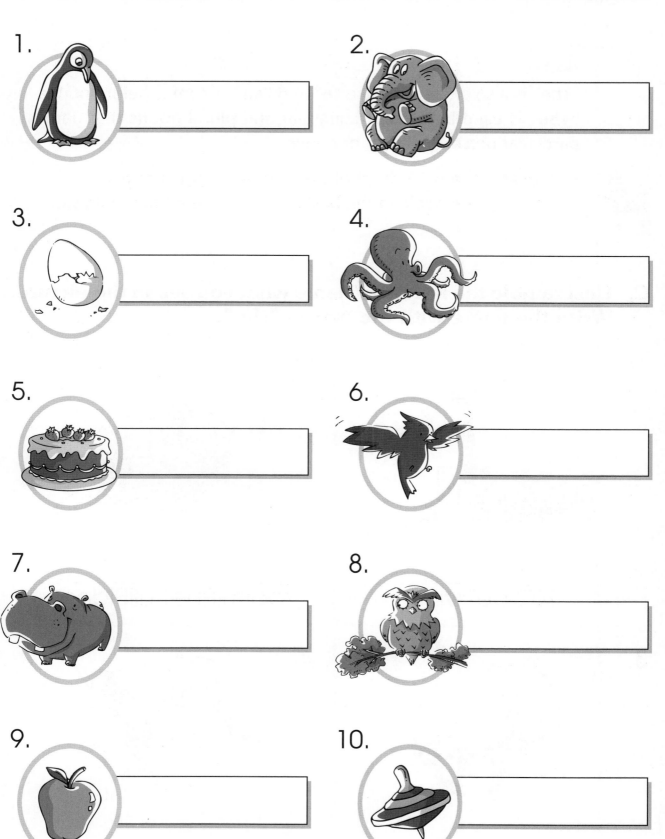

1.

2.

3.

4.

5.

6.

7.

8.

9.

10.

ISBN: 978-1-897457-01-6

### The

"The" is also an article.  Like "a" and "an", it comes before nouns. "**The**" is used before both singular and plural nouns that name particular persons, places, or things.

*Examples*:  the car in front of the house     the Internet
          the apple in the basket          the Prime Minister

**C.  Unscramble the letters to name what you see in the picture. Write the name with the article "the".**

1.

_____
NC oeTwr

2.

_____
raaimlPnet uiiBldngs

3.

_____
Gerta skaeL

4.

_____
diaCnaan glaf

ISBN: 978-1-897457-01-6

**D. Fill in the blanks with the correct articles.**

1. _____ eight planets revolve around _____ sun.

2. _____ Earth is bigger than _____ moon.

3. _____ stars seem to form _____ oval shape.

4. We may see _____ shooting star.

5. _____ moon is the brightest object

   in _____ night sky.

**E. The articles are missing from the sentences below. Rewrite the sentences by adding the correct articles.**

1. Penguin lives in South Pole.

   _____

2. Boy in story is helpful.

   _____

3. You need to buy orange and watermelon.

   _____

4. Parker family visited CNE.

   _____

# unit 5 Verbs (1)

## Verbs

A **verb** is usually an action word.  It tells what someone or something does.

*Example*:    A clown <u>does</u> funny tricks.

## A.  Draw lines to match the verbs with the pictures.

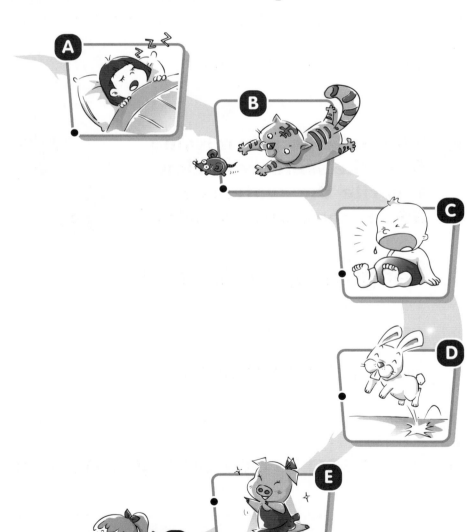

1.  cries    •

2.  hops    •

3.  dances    •

4.  chases    •

5.  sleeps    •

6.  cycles    •

**B. Underline the verbs in the sentences.**

1. This bus goes to the train station.

2. Bees collect nectar from flowers.

3. The chef works in that hotel.

4. Rosanne likes eating tortilla chips.

5. We give presents to one another at Christmas.

**C. Look at the picture.  Write the missing letters to complete the verbs in the sentences.**

1. Some children s___i___ in the sea.

2. A boy and a girl p___ ___y a ball game.

3. A dog r___ ___s after Sam.

4. Chris bu___ ___ds a sandcastle.

## Am, Is, and Are

"**Am**" is used with "**I**".

"**Is**" is used to tell about one person, animal, place, or thing.

"**Are**" is used to tell about more than one person, animal, place, or thing.

*Examples*: There <u>are</u> two books.
One of them <u>is</u> on the table.

**D.** **Look at the pictures and read the sentences.  Circle ⃝ the correct words.**

1. The birds    am / is / are    singing.

2. The dog    am / is / are    barking.

3. There    am / is / are    a happy face on the vest.

4. I    am / is / are    playing with my cat.

ISBN: 978-1-897457-01-6

**E. Look at the picture. Fill in the blanks with "am", "is", or "are".**

1. There _____ a bike on the roof of the car.

2. I _____ walking behind my dad.

3. There _____ a hive in the tree.

4. The bees _____ flying around the hive.

5. It _____ a sunny day.

6. There _____ some apples in the tree.

7. I _____ waving at my friend.

8. Her dad _____ driving.

**Present Tense Verbs**

A **present tense verb** tells what happens now. Add "s" to the base form of the verb to tell about one person or thing. Use the base form to tell about more than one person or thing.

*Examples*:   My dad <u>works</u> in a community centre.
My two sisters <u>work</u> in the same bank.

## A. Circle ○ the correct verb form for the action in each picture.

1.

act / acts

2.

cook / cooks

3.

hit / hits

4.

collect / collects

**B. Look at each verb on the left. Circle ◯ the noun that goes with it.**

1. **drinks** → the cat      my parents

2. **carry** → the policeman      the girls

3. **play** → a puppy      Zoe and I

4. **hops** → two frogs      the kangaroo

5. **throw** → the players      Dad

**C. Fill in the blank with the correct verb form to complete each sentence.**

1. Grandma and Grandpa _____ a walk in the
   take / takes
   park.

2. This book _____ us many
   tell / tells
   fun facts.

3. Plants _____ sunlight
   need / needs
   and water to grow.

4. He _____ the window
   open / opens
   to let in fresh air.

> **Past Tense Verbs**
>
> A **past tense verb** tells what happened in the past. Most verbs add "d" or "ed" to form the past tense.
>
> *Examples*: bake → baked     climb → climbed

**D. Circle ◯ the past tense verbs in the sentences.**

> Some of them contain no past tense verbs.

1. Oscar likes drawing on the walls.

2. Mrs. Kenford walks her dog every day.

3. The children jumped into the pool at once.

4. Cheryl looked into the box and found the toonie.

5. Let's spend our holiday in Algonquin Park.

6. They can have their lunch in the food court.

7. I tied a bow around the gift box.

8. The girls shared the bag of potato chips.

9. It rained heavily yesterday.

ISBN: 978-1-897457-01-6

**E.** **Read the present tense verbs in Column A. Write them in the past tense in Column B.**

| Column A | Column B |
|---|---|
| 1. dance | _____ |
| 2. pick | _____ |
| 3. save | _____ |
| 4. learn | _____ |

**F.** **Look at the pictures. Fill in the blanks with the past tense verbs in (B).**

1.

They _____ some flowers in the garden.

2.

Rex _____ money for a new video game.

3.

The girl _____ beautifully on the stage.

4.

The baby elephant _____ how to stand.

ISBN: 978-1-897457-01-6

## A. Read the story. Circle ◯ the common nouns and underline the proper nouns.

Ray is a little firefly. He carries a light with him. He lives with his mom and dad near Farmer Sam's farm.

Ray's mom always reminds him, "Never ever lose your light."

"Fireflies without lights are just common beetles," his dad adds.

Ray has four good friends: Jane, Kelly, Ted, and Dave. Jane is a ladybug; Kelly is a cricket; Ted is a cockroach; Dave is a mantis. They like playing together. They also like chatting with Kingsley, Farmer Sam's dog, because he is a wise old dog. He always helps them solve their problems.

It is a fine Monday in June. The five little friends are sitting by a tree log on the grass thinking of what to do.

ISBN: 978-1-897457-01-6

**B. Read the story in (A) again. Find an example of each of the following.**

| Common Noun | Proper Noun |
|---|---|

1. person: _____
2. animal: _____
3. place: _____
4. thing: _____

5. person: _____
6. animal: _____
7. day: _____
8. month: _____

**C. Look at the pictures. Write what they are.**

1. _____

2. _____

3. _____

4. _____

5. _____

ISBN: 978-1-897457-01-6

**D. Fill in the blanks with the correct pronouns.**

"Let's play a game," says Kelly. "What game shall 1._____ play?"

"How about hide and seek?" Dave asks.

Ray doesn't quite like this game. 2._____ asks, "Shall 3._____ play something else? 4._____ can always find me easily because 5._____ carry a light with me."

"Maybe 6._____ can leave your light here on the log. When 7._____ finish the game, 8._____ can come back for it. 9._____ won't walk away on its own, right?" Jane suggests. 10._____ likes playing hide and seek very much, and would like to start the game right away.

So the five friends begin the game. 11._____ play happily near the farm.

ISBN: 978-1-897457-01-6

**E. Circle ○ the correct article(s) to complete each sentence.**

1. Ted is   a / an / the   'it' in
   a / an / the   first game.

2. He sees something moving under   a / an / the   leaf.

3. He turns over   a / an / the   leaf happily but finds
   that it is just   a / an / the   ant.

4. Then he sees   a / an / the   shadow moving
   slightly behind   a / an / the   house of Kingsley
   a / an / the   Dog.

5. He rushes over to see who he finds but discovers that
   it is just   a / an / the   bush swaying in   a / an / the
   wind.

6.   A / An / The   moon is already high up in
   a / an / the   night sky but   a / an / the   game
   is not over yet.

**F. Correct the underlined word in each sentence. All sentences are in the present tense.**

1. Ray <u>are</u> hiding inside a hole in a tree. _____

2. "I <u>is</u> not carrying my light tonight, so Ted _____ won't be able to find me," he <u>think</u>. _____

3. He <u>peek</u> from the tree hole. _____

4. He sees Ted.  He <u>are</u> standing right _____ under the tree.

5. Then he hears some noises.  They <u>comes</u> from behind a fence. _____

6. Ted dashes over there and <u>find</u> both _____ Jane and Kelly.

7. Before long, he <u>pull</u> Dave out from a _____ tunnel in the ground.

8. Ray <u>stay</u> in his hiding place. _____

9. After a long while, he <u>hear</u> his friends _____ call out, "Ray, it <u>are</u> already very late _____ now.  We <u>needs</u> to go home." _____

ISBN: 978-1-897457-01-6

**G. Rewrite the sentences below. Change the present tense verbs to past tense verbs.**

1. Ray is the only one that Ted fails to find.

   _____

   _____

2. Ray suddenly remembers his light.

   _____

   _____

3. He and his friends walk back to the tree log.

   _____

   _____

4. They talk happily about the game on the way.

   _____

   _____

5. When they reach the log, they discover that Ray's light is gone.

   _____

   _____

   _____

## Adjectives

An **adjective** tells about a noun (person, animal, place, or thing).
It often tells how a person, an animal, a place, or a thing looks.

*Examples*:   a <u>tall</u> girl (a person)
a <u>cute</u> cat (an animal)
a <u>big</u> park (a place)
a <u>sharp</u> pencil (a thing)

## A.   Draw lines to match the adjectives with the nouns.

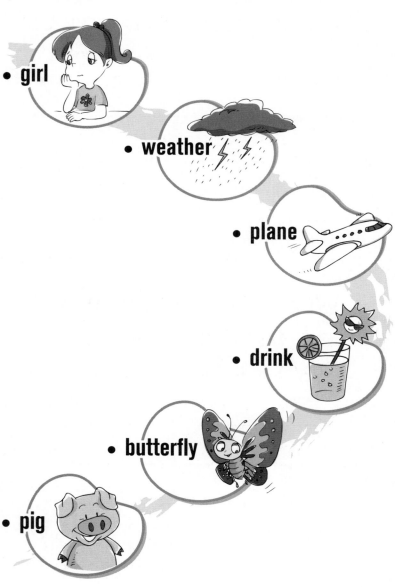

• girl

• weather

• plane

• drink

• butterfly

• pig

1. sad        •

2. cold       •

3. beautiful  •

4. stormy     •

5. fast       •

6. fat        •

ISBN: 978-1-897457-01-6

**B. Look at each picture. Find an adjective from the list that tells about the noun. Write it on the line.**

slow    fierce    bright    long

1.

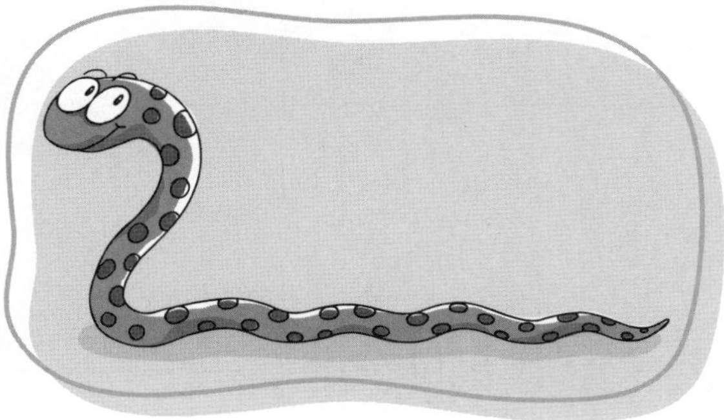

a _____ snake

2.

a _____ dog

3.

a _____ snail

4.

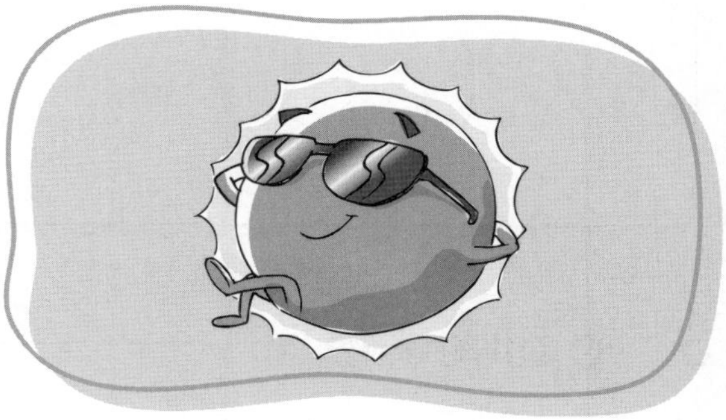

a _____ sun

**C. Look at each picture. Write an adjective to tell about it.**

1.

a _____
kitten

2.

a _____
chick

3.

a _____
Christmas tree

ISBN: 978-1-897457-01-6

Some adjectives tell the colour or number of people, animals, places, or things.

*Examples*:   the <u>blue</u> sky
   <u>three</u> strawberries

## D. Colour or draw the pictures.

1. a yellow mango

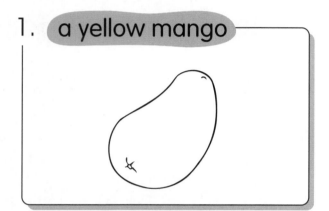

2. two lollipops

3. a blue kite

4. four stars

5. a brown teddy bear

6. five apples

ISBN: 978-1-897457-01-6

Some adjectives tell the size or shape of nouns.

*Examples*:  a <u>big</u> whale
an <u>oval</u> balloon

**E.  Look at each picture.  Find an adjective from the list that tells about the noun.  Write what it is on the line.**

**Adjectives**

huge
tiny
round
square
oval

**Nouns**

bee
globe
dish
bear
mirror

1.  an _____

2.  _____

3.  _____

4.  _____

5.  _____

ISBN: 978-1-897457-01-6

## Location Words

A **location word** tells where a person, an animal, a place, or a thing is located.

*Examples*: The cat is <u>behind</u> the TV.
The mouse is <u>beside</u> the TV.

## A. Write the correct location word for each picture.

> in   on   beside   behind   above   under

1.

_____

2.

_____

3.

_____

4.

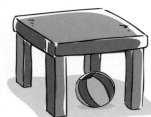

_____

5.

_____

6.

_____

ISBN: 978-1-897457-01-6

**B. Look at the pictures.  Fill in the blanks with the correct location words to complete the sentences.**

1.

The cats are sleeping _____ the couch.

2.

How many monkeys are there _____ the cage?

3.

The sunflowers _____ the fence are tall.

4.

The tree house is high _____ the ground.

5.

The shoes _____ the boots belong to me.

6.

The girls sit _____ the colourful beach umbrella.

## C. Read the directions and complete the picture.

- Draw a bird flying above the tree.
- Draw a girl sitting under the tree.
- Draw a boy playing on the swing.
- Draw a box on the grass.
- Draw a cat in the box.
- Draw a fountain behind the bushes.
- Draw some flowers beside the rock.
- Colour the picture.

**D. Look at the picture. Write sentences with the given location words.**

1. in _____

_____

2. on _____

_____

3. beside _____

_____

4. behind _____

_____

5. above _____

_____

6. under _____

_____

**Sentences**

A **sentence** is a group of words. It tells a complete thought about someone or something. A sentence begins with a capital letter and ends with a period (.).

*Example*: We like playing basketball.

**A. Read each group of words. Colour ☺ if it forms a sentence. Colour ☹ if it does not.**

1. The little kitten.                    ☺   ☹

2. Grandma is baking muffins.           ☺   ☹

3. Nina gives.                          ☺   ☹

4. They work out in the gym.            ☺   ☹

5. Is delicious.                        ☺   ☹

6. Jake wants to win the race.          ☺   ☹

7. Corn on the cob.                     ☺   ☹

8. Penguins live in cold weather.       ☺   ☹

ISBN: 978-1-897457-01-6

**B. Read the sentences. Match them with the correct pictures by writing the letters in the boxes.**

A Carrie doesn't know the answer.

B The boy has a funny mask.

C The house looks scary.

D Pandas like bamboo shoots.

E The children are cheering loudly.

1. □

2. □

3. □

4. □

5. □

**C. Rewrite the following as sentences.**

1. i like chewing gum

_____

2. we buy gum in a candy shop

_____

3. bubble gum has many flavours

_____

> ### The Subject of a Sentence
>
> The **subject** tells whom or what the sentence is about.
>
> *Example*:  Dolphins live in the sea.
>
> In this sentence, "dolphins" is the subject.

**D. Underline the subject in each sentence.**

1. Grandpa and Grandma are visiting us this winter.

2. The school bus stops in front of the house.

3. Monkeys like swinging from tree to tree.

4. Nina hid the lollipop under her pillow.

5. The duck is quacking loudly.

6. Rome is the capital of Italy.

7. Summer starts in June.

8. Zeta and Alice walk their dog together after school.

9. The aliens fly the spaceship.

ISBN: 978-1-897457-01-6

**E. Draw a line to match each subject with the rest of the sentence.**

1.

The balloon •

2.
The ladybug •

3.
The clock •

4.
The CN Tower •

• **A** is ticking loudly.

• **B** is very tiny.

• **C** is up in the sky.

• **D** is in Toronto.

**F. Look at each picture and complete the sentence.**

1. 2. 3.

1. The clown _____ .

2. The frog _____ .

3. Dad _____ .

ISBN: 978-1-897457-01-6

**Telling Sentences**

A **telling sentence** tells about someone or something. It begins with a capital letter and ends with a period (.).

*Example*: The snowman has a scarf.

## A. Colour the box if it is a telling sentence.

1. They slept in the tent at night. ☐

2. Stanley Park is in Vancouver. ☐

3. What's that in your hand? ☐

4. Are you serious? ☐

5. How lovely! ☐

6. They went fishing. ☐

7. Why are you crying? ☐

8. It is rainy today. ☐

9. Cecil likes dinosaurs. ☐

ISBN: 978-1-897457-01-6

## Asking Sentences

An **asking sentence** asks about someone or something. It begins with a capital letter and ends with a question mark (?).

*Example*: How much is the teddy bear?

**B.** Check ✔ the box if it is an asking sentence. Put a cross ✘ in the box if it is not.

1. How awesome! ☐

2. Do you like skiing? ☐

3. The rabbit has red eyes. ☐

4. Why are you so sad? ☐

5. I don't know what to do. ☐

6. Hurry, or you'll be late! ☐

7. What can we buy in that shop? ☐

8. Are you joining the charity walk? ☐

9. How can we get down? ☐

## Surprising Sentences

A **surprising sentence** shows strong emotion like fear, anger, or excitement. It begins with a capital letter and ends with an exclamation mark (!).

*Example*:   Wow!  It's gorgeous!

**C.  Write "S" in the circle if it is a surprising sentence.**

1.  We finally won!  ◯

2.  Can somebody help me?  ◯

3.  Let's go.  ◯

4.  The children are in the park.  ◯

5.  How pretty!  ◯

6.  Come here.  ◯

7.  Is it true?  ◯

8.  Help!  ◯

9.  Ouch!  It hurts!  ◯

ISBN: 978-1-897457-01-6

**D. Look at the picture. Write what each person is saying using the punctuation mark in the ⬭ to end the sentence. Then write what type of sentence it is in the box.**

1. _____

    _____

2. _____

    _____

3. _____

    _____

4. _____

    _____

ISBN: 978-1-897457-01-6

## Punctuation

All sentences end with **punctuation marks**.

- A telling sentence ends with a period (.).
  *Example*:   She is my friend.

- An asking sentence ends with a question mark (?).
  *Example*:   Where's Celia?

- A surprising sentence ends with an exclamation mark (!).
  *Example*:   It's incredible!

**A.  Put the correct punctuation in the circles.**

1.  You have my word on this ◯

2.  You did it ◯

3.  Take a look at this ◯

4.  See you ◯

5.  I'll be back in an hour ◯

6.  What's up ◯

7.  Can you imagine that ◯

8.  It's just awesome ◯

9.  How ridiculous ◯

ISBN: 978-1-897457-01-6

**B. Check ✔ the box if the sentence ends with the correct punctuation. Circle ◯ the wrong punctuation and put the correct one above it.**

1. What an awful thing? ☐

2. How did you do that? ☐

3. A baby dog is called a puppy! ☐

4. There are two stories in this book. ☐

5. What she wants is hot chocolate? ☐

6. Is it far away from here. ☐

7. Why is that so! ☐

8. He wants to be an artist. ☐

9. Watch out. ☐

10. How lovely! ☐

ISBN: 978-1-897457-01-6

## Capitalization

All proper nouns begin with capital letters.
All sentences begin with capital letters.

*Examples*:  The Wizard of Oz is an interesting story.
Kyle likes this story very much.

**C.  Rewrite the words with capital letters if needed.**

1.  aunt stella

_____

2.  my teacher

_____

3.  lake ontario

_____

4.  police officer

_____

5.  pet store

_____

6.  monkey

_____

7.  shoppers drug mart

_____

8.  toronto zoo

_____

9.  monday

_____

10.  storybooks

_____

ISBN: 978-1-897457-01-6

**D. Follow the rules of capitalization and rewrite the sentences.**

1. tyra named her dog casey.

   _____

   _____

2. thanksgiving day is in october.

   _____

3. ian lives on scottfield crescent.

   _____

4. how did jason get the key?

   _____

5. my sister was sick last thursday.

   _____

6. the gardners went to italy for a holiday.

   _____

   _____

7. roald dahl wrote "charlie and the chocolate factory".

   _____

   _____

ISBN: 978-1-897457-01-6

## Word Order

Sentences need to make sense. The order of the words in a sentence can change the meaning of the sentence.

*Examples*:   The dog ate the bone.
The bone ate the dog.

**A. Read each pair of sentences. Check ✔ the one that makes sense.**

1. The car stole the robbers. ☐

   The robbers stole the car. ☐

2. Jamie put the cat in the basket. ☐

   Jamie put the basket in the cat. ☐

3. The table is sitting at the children. ☐

   The children are sitting at the table. ☐

4. Sharon turned on the computer. ☐

   The computer turned on Sharon. ☐

5. My sister goes to Westside School. ☐

   Westside School goes to my sister. ☐

ISBN: 978-1-897457-01-6

**B. Look at each pair of pictures. Colour the one that makes sense. Then write a sentence to go with it.**

1.

2.

3.

**C. Look at the picture.  Rewrite the sentences so that they make sense.**

1.  The sky is in a bird.

    _____

2.  There is a farm on the farmhouse.

    _____

3.  The chicks are feeding Smith.

    _____

4.  Big baskets have the boys.

    _____

5.  Some potatoes have collected Jerry.

    _____

    _____

**D. Put the words in order to make sentences.**

1. ate    ice cream    an    Sally    cone

   _____

   _____

2. are    at    They    rink    skating    the

   _____

   _____

3. to    need    chest    open    key    a    You    the

   _____

   _____

4. toy    Dad    for    car    me    bought    a

   _____

   _____

5. The    sleeping    couch    on    puppy    is    the

   _____

   _____

# unit 13 Synonyms and Antonyms

## Synonyms

**Synonyms** are words that mean the same.

*Examples*:  big – large
fast – quick
price – cost

**A.  Colour ☺ if they are synonyms.  Colour ☹ if they are not.**

1.  stop – halt

2.  year – calendar

3.  smooth – rugged

4.  thin – slim

5.  dish – plate

6.  right – correct

7.  colour – green

8.  sand – rock

9.  pretty – beautiful

ISBN: 978-1-897457-01-6

**B.** Circle ◯ the word that is a synonym for each word on the left.

1. **happy** ➡ sad     smile     glad     cheer

2. **tall** ➡ thin     high     above     short

3. **windy** ➡ blow     rainy     breezy     gust

4. **jump** ➡ hop     dance     stand     sit

5. **dark** ➡ black     dim     bright     light

**C.** Rewrite each sentence by replacing the underlined word with its synonym.

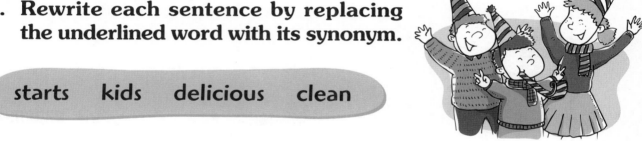

starts     kids     delicious     clean

1. The <u>children</u> have fun at the party.

   _____

2. Your room is really <u>tidy</u>.

   _____

3. The show <u>begins</u> at eight o'clock.

   _____

4. This ice cream is so <u>yummy</u>!

   _____

## Antonyms

**Antonyms** are words that mean the opposite.

*Examples*:  big – small
fast – slow
love – hate

**D.  Draw lines to join the words in the boxes to the pictures and match the antonyms.**

1.

2.

3.

4.

5.

| tall |
| old |
| cheap |
| dirty |
| full |

- expensive
- short
- hungry
- young
- clean

ISBN: 978-1-897457-01-6

# E. Complete the crossword puzzle with antonyms of the clue words.

## Across

A. huge
B. quickly
C. push
D. alone
E. light

## Down

1. easy
2. weak
3. stop
4. sad
5. rotten

## A. Read the story. Circle ○ the adjectives.

Ray plays with his four good friends all night. However, the happy night turns into a terrible one for Ray. His light is lost! It's no longer there <u>on the log</u>. Where can it be?

Ray and his friends start searching for the missing light. They look <u>under the old tree</u>. No light! They get to a nest in the tall tree. There are just three eggs <u>in the nest</u>. No light is there! They look <u>behind the wooden fence</u>. It's not there! They begin to lose hope.

Then Kelly suddenly remembers wise Kingsley, Farmer Sam's dog. He should be able to help them find the light. They rush to the farm at once.

Kingsley's doghouse is <u>beside the red mailbox</u> in front of the farmhouse. The moon is right <u>above the farmhouse</u>. It's late in the night and Kingsley is sound asleep.

ISBN: 978-1-897457-01-6

**B. Look at the underlined words in (A) again. Fill in the blanks with the location words. Then check ✔ the correct box in each picture to show the location.**

1. _____ the log

2. _____ the tree

3. _____ the nest

4. _____ the fence

5. _____ the mailbox

6. _____ the farmhouse

**C. Read the paragraph below. Copy the complete sentences on the lines. Then circle ○ the subject of each sentence.**

Ray and his friends wake Kingsley up. A big yawn. Kingsley asks them what happened. They tell him that Ray's light is lost. Is big problem. Kingsley sits there and closes his eyes. He doesn't speak for a long while. Ray quietly. Then a big smile appears on his face. He opens his eyes. Five little friends. He seems to have found a solution to the problem. Ray looks eagerly at him.

_____

_____

_____

_____

_____

_____

_____

_____

ISBN: 978-1-897457-01-6

**D. Rewrite each sentence using the correct capitalization and punctuation. Then write "T" (telling), "A" (asking), or "S" (surprising) in the box to show the type of sentence.**

1. do you know where my light is, kingsley

   _____  ☐

2. can you think of anyone that likes lights

   _____  ☐

3. is it molly the moth

   _____  ☐

4. the five friends ask in unison

   _____  ☐

5. where does molly live

   _____  ☐

6. she lives in farmer sam's barn

   _____  ☐

7. kingsley, how clever
   you are  ☐

   _____

   _____

   _____

**E. The sentences below do not make sense. Rewrite each sentence by changing the positions of the underlined words. Make other necessary changes.**

1. <u>The barn</u> gets to <u>the five friends</u> at once.

   _____

   _____

2. <u>Molly's table</u> is right there in the middle of <u>Ray's light</u>.

   _____

   _____

3. <u>A warm glow</u> is giving out <u>the light</u>.

   _____

   _____

4. <u>Ray's light</u> is so happy to see <u>the little friends</u> again.

   _____

   _____

5. <u>His light</u> has never found <u>Ray</u> so beautiful.

   _____

   _____

ISBN: 978-1-897457-01-6

**F. Fill in each blank with a synonym (S) or an antonym (A) of the given word.**

"Oh, is this your light?" Molly 1._____ . "Yes, it's
answers (A)

mine," Ray says. "Sorry, I thought it belonged to no

one. You all know how much I 2._____ lights. I
hate (A)

was taking a walk near the farm when I saw the light

on the log. It's so 3._____ . I just couldn't take my
pretty (S)

eyes off it. I felt quite sure that nobody would

4._____ to get it, so I took it home," Molly explains.
go (A)

Ray is so 5._____ to have found his light. When
happy (S)

he reaches home, his mom and dad ask, "Why are

you so 6._____ ?" Ray smiles and says, "I lost
early (A)

something precious, but now I've found it. I'll never

let myself 7._____ it again!"
find (A)

ISBN: 978-1-897457-01-6

We are cheery birds.

cheery

ISBN: 978-1-897457-01-6

# 1 The Rainbow

Today, when I got out of school, I saw a beautiful rainbow. The colours of the rainbow were <u>yellow</u>, <u>orange</u>, <u>red</u>, <u>blue</u>, and <u>purple</u>.

Some people say that there is a pot of <u>gold</u> at the end of a rainbow. Also, some people say that a rainbow means good luck.

What do you think?

**A. Some of the words in the passage are colour words. Write them on the lines below.**

1. __ __ __          2. __ __ __ __ __ __

3. __ __ __ __          4. __ __ __ __ __

5. __ __ __ __          6. __ __ __ __ __ __

**One of the colours above is also the name for a metal that is worth a lot of money. What is it?**

⊙ __ ⊙ __ ⊙ __ ⊙ __

*Can you think of another word that is both a metal and the name of coins?*

⊙ __ ⊙ __ ⊙ __ ⊙ __ ⊙ __ ⊙ __

ISBN: 978-1-897457-01-6

**B. Use the words in the passage to help you fill in the blanks in the sentences.**

1. The name I give to this day is __ __ __ __ __ .

2. In many pictures, the sun looks __ __ __ __ __ __ .

3. The colour that rhymes with "bed" is __ __ __ .

4. __ __ __ __ __ __ is a fruit and also a colour.

5. I am in a pot at the end of a rainbow.

   I am __ __ __ __ .

6. The sky is __ __ __ __ .

**C. Look at each picture. Write the correct word on the lines.**

1.

   ____

2.

   _____

3.

   good _____

4.

   _____

5.

   _____

6.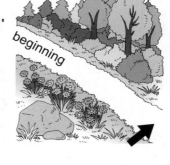

   _____

**D.** Find the word in "The Rainbow" that rhymes with (sounds the same as) each picture.

1.

——  ——  ——  ——

2.

——  ——  ——  ——

3.

——  ——  ——  ——

4.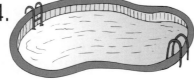

——  ——  ——  ——

5.

——  ——  ——  ——

6.

——  ——  ——  ——

**E.** Circle the words in the Rainbow Word Search.

**Rainbow Word Search**

```
b c g o k e m p r m s u t
m t o d a y s g h y q c b
d v l o l j t f m b m d h
c e d l g i b p l r b j q
f p j a s v k y e l l o w
h u n o i r e x s o u d c
o r a n g e n j d y e g t
i p m b s d f t p h a k l
c l d p h u z m l w r m f
l e j g q n a o k e l c n
```

red
blue
gold
orange
yellow
purple
today

ISBN: 978-1-897457-01-6

**F.** Each rainbow has one of the words in the word bank. Sort the letters and write the word on the lines below the rainbow.

| people | school | blue | purple |
|--------|--------|------|--------|
| orange | yellow | luck | gold |

1. r l p e u p

_ _ _ _ _ _

2. l o h o c s

_ _ _ _ _ _

3. o e g r a n

_ _ _ _ _ _

4. u l c k

_ _ _ _

5. l w y l e o

_ _ _ _ _ _

6. b e l u

_ _ _ _

7. o p e l p e

_ _ _ _ _ _

8. o d l g

_ _ _ _

Last Saturday, my <u>dad</u> took my <u>sister</u> and me to a <u>farm</u>. It was a small farm near our <u>city</u>.

The farm had a <u>barn</u>, cows, pigs, hens, and chicks. There was also a rooster. There was a pretty pond on the farm with ducks in it.

Before we left, we bought some fresh eggs and cheese.

**A.** **Each of the following clues tells about one of the underlined words in the passage. Write it on the lines.**

1. I am the father in a family.

   — — —

2. I am a place where cows and ducks live.

   — — — —

3. I am a place with tall buildings, highways, stores, and houses.

   — — — —

4. I am a house for cows and horses.

   — — — —

5. I am the female opposite of brother.

   — — — — —

**B.** Read the clues for the crossword puzzle.  Use the word bank to help you fill in the answers.

**Across**

A. pool of water
B. baby chickens
C. big animals that give milk

**Down**

1. animals that give us eggs
2. place where you find big and tall buildings
3. animals that say "oink"
4. house for cows and horses

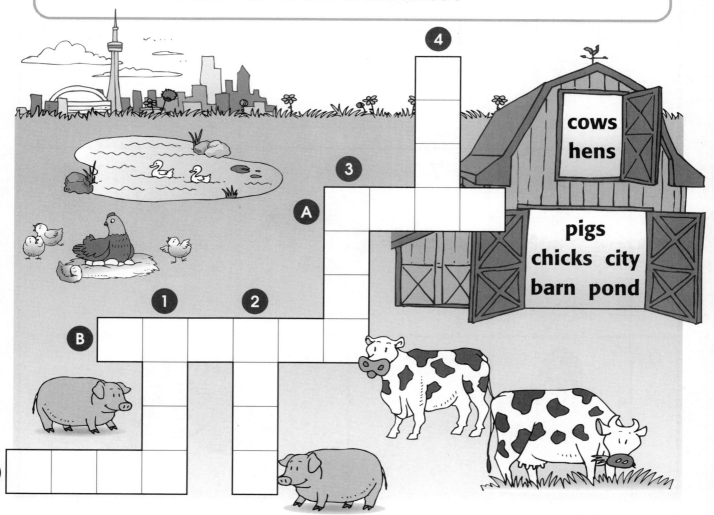

cows
hens

pigs
chicks  city
barn  pond

## C. Circle the animals that live on or things that belong to a farm. Write the words on the lines.

duck    chick    pond    cheese    city
tractor    pig    toys    barn    rooster

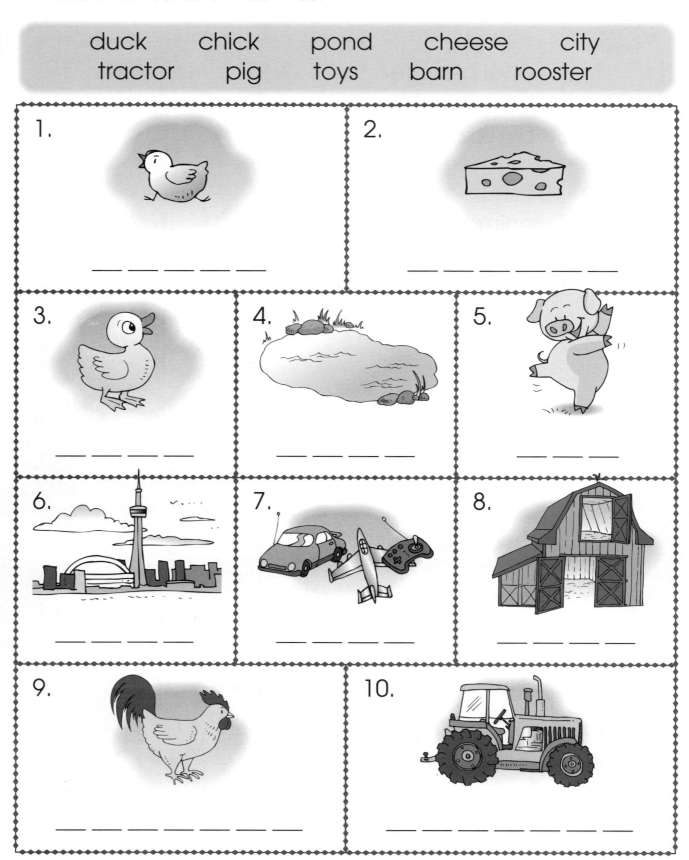

1. _____

2. _____

3. _____

4. _____

5. _____

6. _____

7. _____

8. _____

9. _____

10. _____

ISBN: 978-1-897457-01-6

**D. Name the things in the pictures. Draw a line to match the two things that rhyme.**

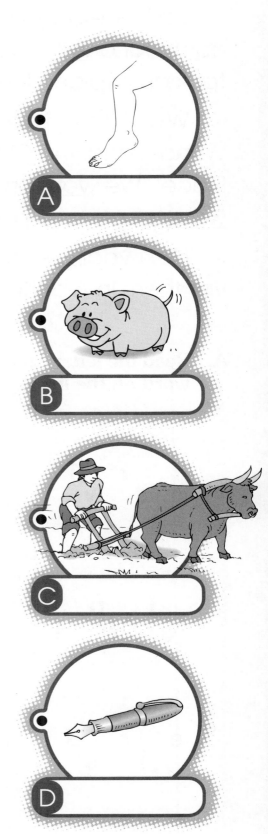

# 3 The Visit

Last week, my <u>aunt</u>, <u>uncle</u>, and <u>cousins</u> came for a <u>visit</u>.  They live in Alberta.  They took an <u>airplane</u> to get here.

We took them to Canada's Wonderland, the CN Tower, and Ontario Place.  We <u>went</u> on roller coaster <u>rides</u>, <u>wave</u> pools, and paddle boats.

Next year, we are going to visit them in Alberta.

**A.** Read the letters in each box below.  Unscramble them and write the word on the lines.

The words are underlined in the passage.

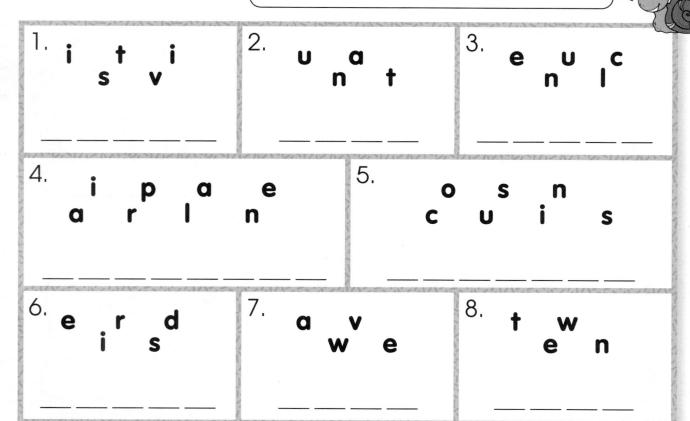

1.  i  t  i
    s     v

\_ \_ \_ \_ \_

2.  u  a
    n     t

\_ \_ \_ \_

3.  e  u  c
    n     l

\_ \_ \_ \_ \_

4.  i     p     a     e
    a     r     l     n

\_ \_ \_ \_ \_ \_ \_ \_

5.  o     s     n
    c  u  i     s

\_ \_ \_ \_ \_ \_ \_

6.  e  r  d
    i     s

\_ \_ \_ \_ \_

7.  a     v
    w  e

\_ \_ \_ \_

8.  t     w
    e     n

\_ \_ \_ \_

ISBN: 978-1-897457-01-6

**B. Look at each picture. Write the word. Use the Word Bank to help you.**

1. _____

2. _____

3. _____

4. _____

5. _____

6. _____

7. _____

8. _____

9. _____

10. _____

11. _____

12. _____

September

| Sun | Mon | Tue | Wed | Thu | Fri | Sat |
|-----|-----|-----|-----|-----|-----|-----|

2004  Popular Calendar

| Jan | Feb | Mar | Apr |
|-----|-----|-----|-----|
| May | Jun | Jul | Aug |
| Sep | Oct | Nov | Dec |

## Word Bank

pool   week   uncle   cousins   boat   year

tree   cat   airplane   aunt   tower   paddle

**C.** **Bella is hiking to the campsite.  Write the word that names each picture along the way.**

1.

2.

3.

4.

### Word Bank

lake     net     tent     boat     pool

boot     fire     duck     bug     nest

8.

7.

6.

5.

9.

10.

**D. Look at the pictures. Read the sentences. Colour the pictures that make sense.**

1. 
| The man drove the car. | The car drove the man. |
|---|---|

2. 
| The tree climbed the cat. | The cat climbed the tree. |
|---|---|

3. 
| The bike rode a boy. | The boy rode a bike. |
|---|---|

4. 
| The dog ate the bone. | The bone ate the dog. |
|---|---|

# 4 The New Pet

On Thursday, my mom and I went to the animal shelter. That is the place where dogs and cats are kept until they get adopted. There are some other kinds of animals there too.

We picked out a beautiful orange and brown tabby cat. We learned that all orange-coloured cats are male! Our new cat is named Tuffy.

**A.** This story takes place on a Thursday. Can you write all the days of the week?

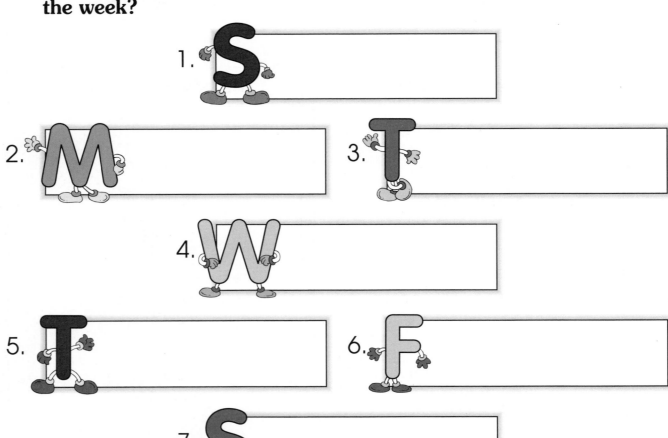

1. S

2. M

3. T

4. W

5. T

6. F

7. S

ISBN: 978-1-897457-01-6

**B.** This story is about getting a pet. Match the names with the animals by writing the letters in the boxes. Colour the animals that can be pets.

A. cat     B. crocodile     C. pig     D. elephant
E. puppy     F. parrot     G. snake     H. zebra
I. canary     J. mouse     K. deer     L. squirrel

1.

2.

3.

4.

5.

6.

7.

8.

9.

10.

11.

12.

**C.** Look at the letters in each doghouse. Unscramble them and write the word on the line. Use the word bank to help you.

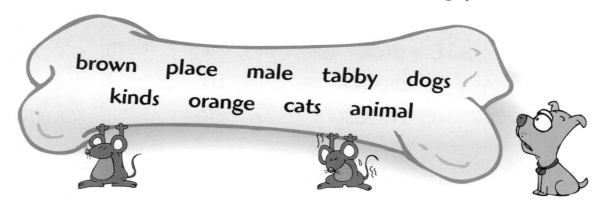

brown  place  male  tabby  dogs
kinds  orange  cats  animal

1.

d  o
s  g

_____

2.

a  i  n
l  m
a

_____

3.

c  a
t  s

_____

4.

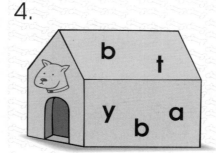

b  t
y  a
b

_____

5.

r  w
b  o
n

_____

6.

p  c
l  e
a

_____

7.

e  a  o
r  g  n

_____

8.

n  i
k  d
s

_____

9.

a  e
m  l

_____

ISBN: 978-1-897457-01-6

Words that rhyme sound the same at the end.
Example:    h**and**    b**and**

**D.** **Say each word in Column A. Find the word that rhymes in Column B. Draw a line to match them.**

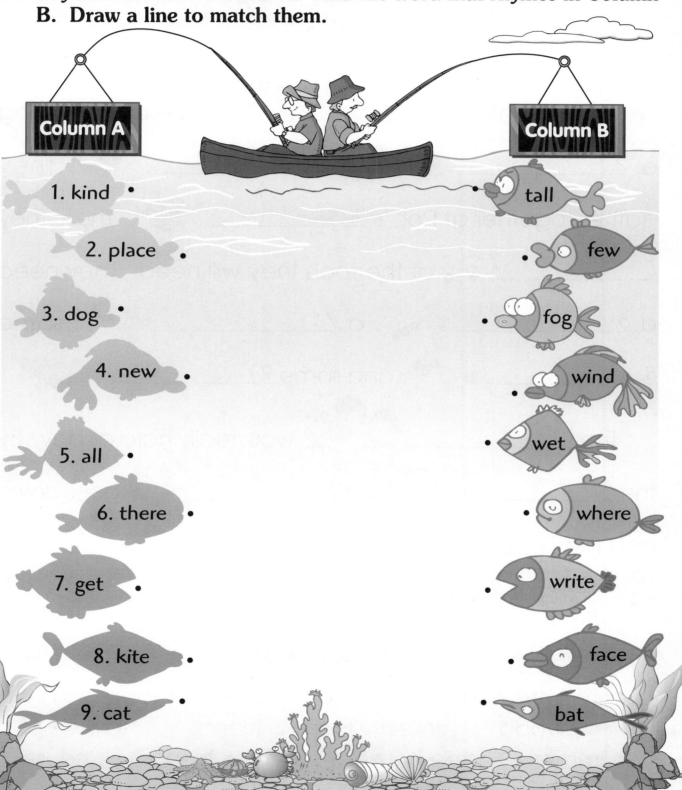

Column A

1. kind
2. place
3. dog
4. new
5. all
6. there
7. get
8. kite
9. cat

Column B

tall
few
fog
wind
wet
where
write
face
bat

**A.** Read the story. Use the pictures and the Word Bank to help you write the words in the blanks.

Rob and his 1._____ are busy building

a 2._____ : 3._____ **1 st** , they

gather together at Rob's 4._____ . Then, they

5._____ at the tools they will need. They need

a 6._____ , a 7._____ , some

8._____ , and some 9._____ .

The 10._____ work really hard all day. By

the 11._____ the 12._____ goes down

and the 13._____ comes up, the 14._____

is finished!

**Word Bank**

tree-house    look    nails    moon

wood    time    First    friends    saw

hammer    tree-house    sun    friends    house

ISBN: 978-1-897457-01-6

The story "The Tree-House" is a **rebus** or picture story. The pictures are in the place of words that name them.

## B. Draw lines to match the words with the pictures.

1.

3.

5.

7.

9.

nails

saw

wood

tree

house

moon

sun

time

hammer

friends

2.

4.

6.

8.

10.

ISBN: 978-1-897457-01-6

**C.** Inside each tool box, there is a word from the story "The Tree-House". Write the word on the line below.

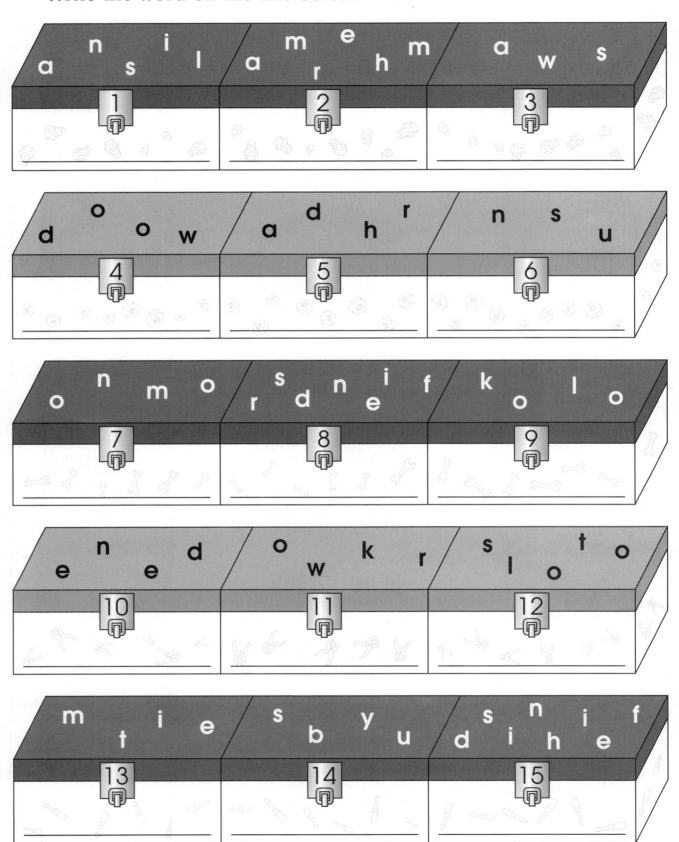

ISBN: 978-1-897457-01-6

**D.** Each of the clues below tells about a word that is related to building. Use the clues and the Word Bank to help you complete the Building Crossword Puzzle.

## Across

A. It drives nails into wood.
B. Sharp metal spikes used with a hammer to hold wood together
C. What hammers and saws are

## Down

1. Tools are what you ___ to build something.
2. A wooden hammer
3. It cuts wood.

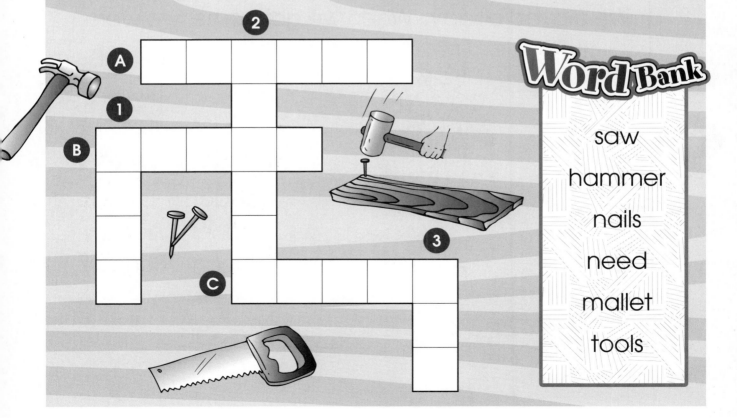

**Word Bank**

saw

hammer

nails

need

mallet

tools

# 6 At the Beach

**A.** Read the story.  Rewrite the jumbled words in the boxes on the lines below.  Use the Word Bank to help you.

On 1. _____ `u d a S n y` , we went to the

2. _____ `c b a e h` with our 3. _____

`i f r n e d s` , David and Colleen.  We took our

4. _____ `u l c n h` and a

beach ball.

The sun was hot, the 5. _____ `a d s n` was

white, and the 6. _____ `n e o c a` was blue.

We played all day.  When we got home, we were

so tired.

## WORD BANK

| | |
|---|---|
| beach | friends |
| sand | ocean |
| lunch | Sunday |

ISBN: 978-1-897457-01-6

**B.** Look at each picture. Write the word that names it on the lines below. Use the Word Bank to help you.

1. ___ ___ ___

2. ___ ___ ___ ___

3. ___ ___ ___ ___

4. ___ ___ ___

5. ___ ___ ___ ___ ___

6. ___ ___ ___

7. ___ ___ ___ ___ ___ ___ ___

8. ___ ___ ___

9. ___ ___ ___ ___

## Word Bank

friends    swim    sand    sky

sun    beach    sea    ball    lunch

## C. Use each of the words in a sentence.

**Example:** sun – The sun is shining today.

A **sentence** begins with a capital letter and ends with a period.

1. beach _____

2. ocean _____

3. friends _____

4. lunch _____

5. sand _____

6. Sunday _____

## Challenge

Choose your own word and put it in a sentence.

ISBN: 978-1-897457-01-6

**D.** Read each clue. Complete the Beach Crossword Puzzle. Use the Word Bank to help you.

*All the clues tell about things you see at the beach.*

# Beach Crossword Puzzle

## Across

A. When the temperature is high, it is ___ .

B. The first day of the week

C. Place where you play in the sand

## Down

1. Colour of the sea and the sky

2. The meal you eat in the middle of the day

3. Very big sea

**Word Bank**

Sunday    blue

ocean    hot

beach    lunch

ISBN: 978-1-897457-01-6

# 7 Bill and Bob

Bill and Bob are twins. This means that they were born on the same day, about the same time, from the same mom. Today is their birthday. They are both six years old. They are brothers.

Bill and Bob like some of the same things. They like to swim and skate. They also like different things. Bob likes to draw and Bill likes to play video games.

Best of all, Bill and Bob are good friends who like each other.

**A. Find the words below in the passage "Bill and Bob". Circle them in the passage and colour each word below when you find it.**

twins ◆ day ◆ time ◆ birthday ◆ six ◆ years

brothers ◆ swim ◆ skate ◆ draw ◆ play ◆ friends

**B. Match the words below with the pictures. Write the letters in the circles.**

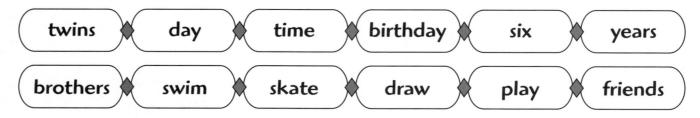

A. brothers    B. friends    C. birthday

D. swim    E. draw    F. skate

G. time    H. play    I. six

J. twins    K. mom    L. video games

ISBN: 978-1-897457-01-6

**C.** Each of these sentences tells about a word in "Bill and Bob". Read the sentence and write the word. Use the Word Bank to help you.

**Example:** <u>B i r t h d a y</u> is the day you were born.

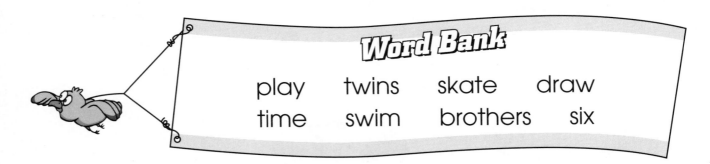

**Word Bank**

play     twins     skate     draw
time     swim     brothers     six

1.  When two babies are born to the same mother on the same day and about the same time, they are called ___ ___ ___ ___ ___ .

2.  A clock tells us the ___ ___ ___ ___ .

3.  The number that comes after five and before seven is ___ ___ ___ .

4.  You can ___ ___ ___ ___ in a pool or a lake.

5.  People ___ ___ ___ ___ ___ on ice.

6.  Bill and Bob are twins and ___ ___ ___ ___ ___ ___ ___ ___ .

7.  Bob likes to ___ ___ ___ ___ .

8.  Bill likes to ___ ___ ___ ___ video games.

ISBN: 978-1-897457-01-6

D. **Read each clue. Complete the crossword puzzle. Use the Word Bank to help you.**

| Across | Down |
|---|---|
| A. Two boys from the same parents | 1. The day you were born |
| B. What a clock tells | 2. How to play on ice |
| C. How old you are is told in ___ . | 3. The number after 5 |

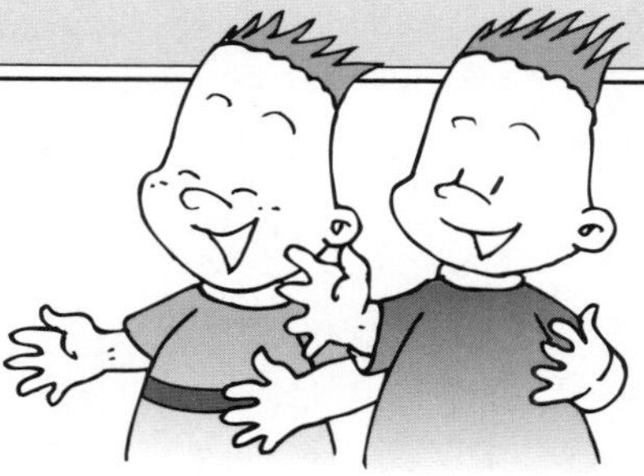

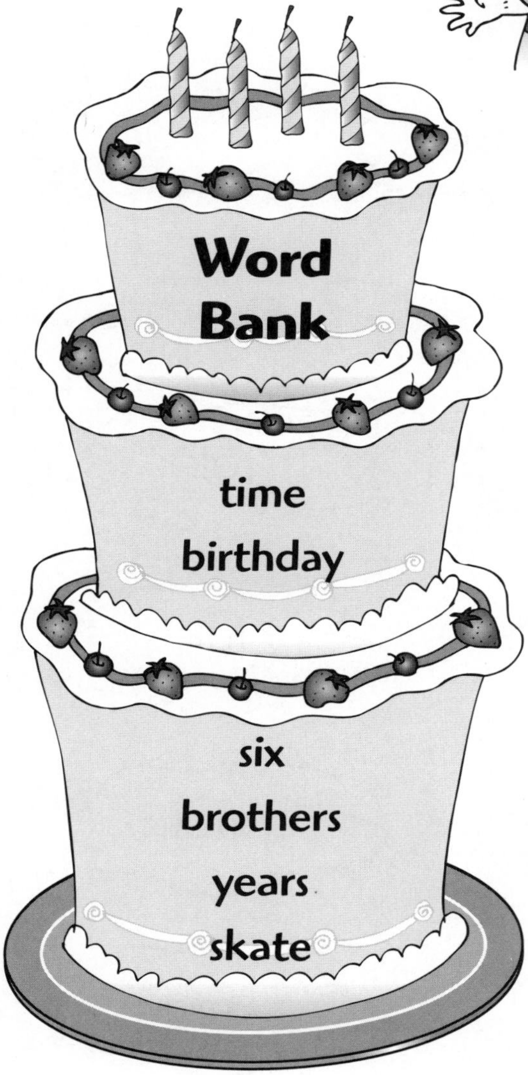

Word Bank
time
birthday
six
brothers
years
skate


2
1
A
B
3
C


ISBN: 978-1-897457-01-6

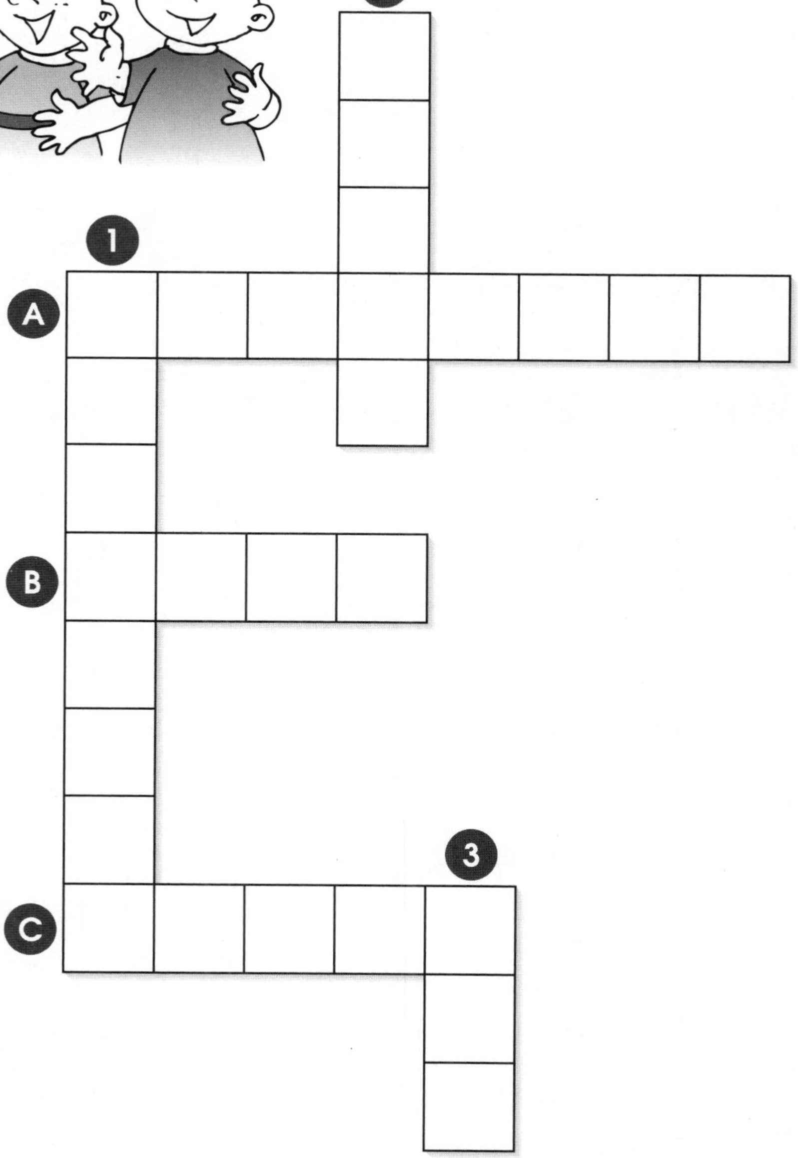

**A.** The word in each frog rhymes with one of the words in the lilypad. Colour each matching pair the same colour.

1. ride
2. bite
3. try
4. run
5. bone
6. dime
7. mile
8. kit
9. pot
10. top
11. bale
12. hug

time    kite    tale

smile    mop    fun

lot    bit    pride

sky    stone    bug

ISBN: 978-1-897457-01-6

**B.** **Fill in the missing word in each sentence. Use the Word Bank to help you.**

Word Bank

tent    boat    airplane
blue    end    ladybug    farm
orange    gold    cow

1. There is a pot of __ __ __ __ at the end of a rainbow.

2. An __ __ __ __ __ __ __ __ travels in the air.

3. The colour that rhymes with "true" is __ __ __ __ .

4. Cheese and milk both come from a __ __ __ .

5. I am a colour and a fruit. I am an __ __ __ __ __ __ .

6. Cows, ducks, and chickens live on a __ __ __ __ .

7. A __ __ __ __ travels on water.

8. The opposite of "beginning" is __ __ __ .

9. A __ __ __ __ __ __ __ is red with black spots.

10. When you go camping, you sleep in a __ __ __ __ .

ISBN: 978-1-897457-01-6

**C.** Dougie the Dog is hunting for bones. The letters in each of these dog bones make a word from the word bank. Unscramble them and write the word on the line.

went    yellow    blue
wave    cows    school    barn
visit    sister    today    farm    boats

1.  l o w y l e

_____

2. d a y t o

_____

3. e l u b

_____

4. c o s o l h

_____

5. a f r m

_____

6. a b r n

_____

7. s t i e r s

_____

8. c w s o

_____

9. o t a b s

_____

10. e t n w

_____

11. a v w e

_____

12. v s t i i

_____

ISBN: 978-1-897457-01-6

**D. Match each word in Column A with its meaning in Column B. Write the letter on the line.**

## Column A

1. tent
2. new
3. male
4. farm
5. pigs
6. uncle
7. Thursday
8. nails
9. saw
10. lunch
11. beach
12. Sunday

## Column B

A. the fifth day of the week

B. the first day of the week

C. place where animals live

D. where you can see the ocean and sand

E. sharp spikes used with a hammer

F. opposite of "female"

G. animals that "oink"

H. opposite of "old"

I. your mom's brother

J. tool used to cut wood

K. meal between breakfast and dinner

L. thing you sleep in when you go camping

| April | | | | | | |
|---|---|---|---|---|---|---|
| Sun | Mon | Tue | Wed | Thu | Fri | Sat |
| | 1 | 2 | 3 | 4 | 5 | 6 |
| 7 | 8 | 9 | 10 | 11 | 12 | 13 |
| 14 | 15 | 16 | 17 | 18 | 19 | 20 |
| 21 | 22 | 23 | 24 | 25 | 26 | 27 |
| 28 | 29 | 30 | | | | |

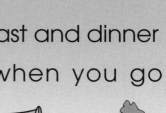

1. _____   2. _____   3. _____   4. _____

5. _____   6. _____   7. _____   8. _____

9. _____   10. _____   11. _____   12. _____

**E.** One of the sentences in each pair does not make sense. Look at the picture. Cross out ✗ the sentence that does not make sense.

1. The dog chewed the bone.

   The bone chewed the dog.

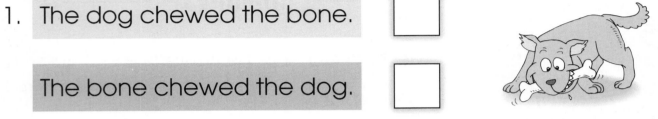

2. The fish ate the whale.

   The whale ate the fish.

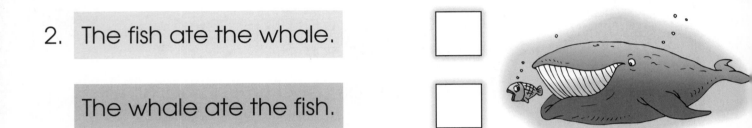

3. The nut ate the squirrel.

   The squirrel ate the nut.

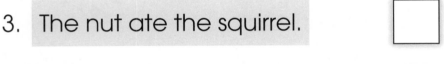
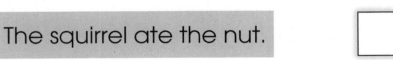

4. The rain fell from the sky.

   The sky fell from the rain.

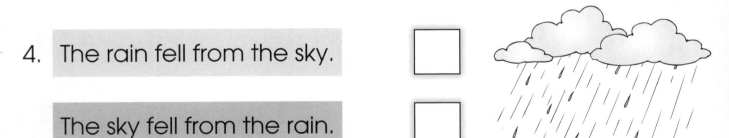

5. The bug crawled on the leaf.

   The leaf crawled on the bug.

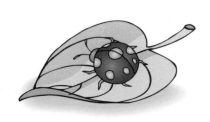

ISBN: 978-1-897457-01-6

**F.** The groom can only reach the bride if he can answer all the clues. Read each clue. Write the letter in the box.

A. not new

B. colour of a banana

C. this day

D. place where you swim

E. hens lay them

F. building where cows live

G. cows give us this

H. animal that gives milk

I. colour of the sky

J. place where you learn

K. place where birds live

L. animal that "mews"

M. colour of an apple

N. opposite of "brother"

O. father in a family

1. sister ☐

2. school ☐

3. yellow ☐

4. today ☐

5. blue ☐

6. tree ☐

7. eggs ☐

8. pool ☐

9. cow ☐

10. dad ☐

11. milk ☐

12. old ☐

13. cat ☐

14. barn ☐

15. red ☐

ISBN: 978-1-897457-01-6

**A.** The story below is written with pictures. Look at each picture and write a sentence that tells about it. Give your story a title.

Title:

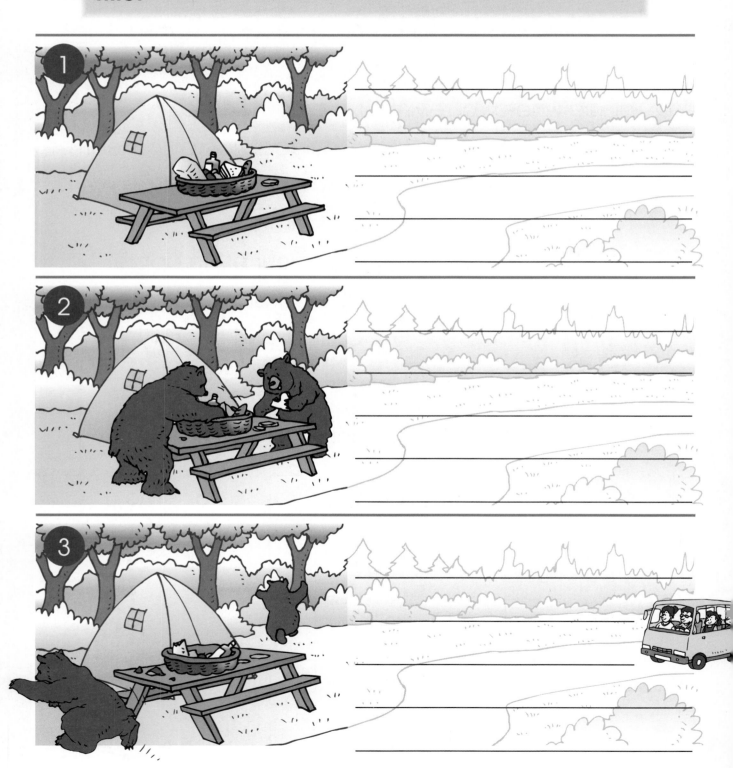

ISBN: 978-1-897457-01-6

**B.** Each line of words below can form a sentence. Put them in order and write the sentence.

1. lots  .  trees  There  of  were

_____

2. family  camping  The  .  went

_____

3. had  tent  sleep  in  .  They  a  to

_____

4. people  sandwiches  ?  like  Do  peanut  butter

_____

5. do  Bears  too  !

_____

6. bears  The  the  ate  food  .

_____

7. picnics  ?  bears  Do  like

_____

**C.** There are words that go with camping in the tent below. Circle them.

trees  chair  tent
kitchen  pegs  pen
car  flap  pot
swim  pillow  picnic
fire  school  table

**D.** The camping words below are all mixed up. Sort them out and write the correct spelling under each tent.

1. e t n t

2. c p m a

3. t e e r

———————  ———————  ———————

4. n i c i c p

5. p e s g

———————————  ———————

6. o f d o

7. f e i r

8. f a p l

———  ———  ———

ISBN: 978-1-897457-01-6

**E.** Look at the picture in each box. Read the sentences. Draw a line through the one that does not fit.

1.

My dad and I like to hike. We have a favourite trail. The treats were good.

2.

My family went on a picnic. The car was dirty. We had peanut butter sandwiches.

3.

Mom and I like to swim. There were lots of caves. We swim in the lake.

4.

Bears like honey. They climb trees to get it. My favourite food is pizza.

# 9 Swimming Fun

**A.** Some words in the story are missing. They are in the Word Bank. Fill in the missing words.

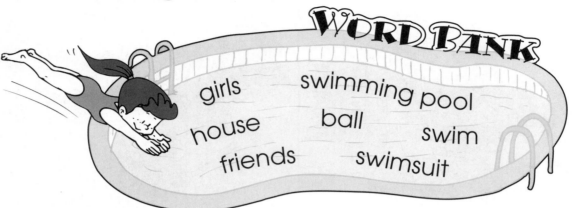

WORD BANK

girls    swimming pool
house    ball    swim
friends    swimsuit

Alexandra changed into her 1.  and got ready

to go for a 2.  in her 3.  . Her two

4.  came over to her 5.  .

The three 6.  jumped into the pool. They

had a huge beach 7.  which they tossed around for

hours. What fun!

1. _____

2. _____    3. _____    4. _____

5. _____    6. _____    7. _____

ISBN: 978-1-897457-01-6

Some words have lots of words that rhyme (sound the same at the end) with them. A good way to find new rhyming words is to go through the letters of the alphabet to see if the letters fit.

**Example:** __ all – <u>b</u>all  <u>c</u>all...

## B. How many more rhyming words can you find?

*You can use capitals to make names too!*

| | | |
|---|---|---|
| 1. __ all | 2. __ im | 3. __ in |
| __ all | __ im | __ in |
| __ all | __ im | __ in |
| __ all | __ im | __ in |
| __ all | __ im | __ in |
| __ all | __ im | __ in |
| 4. __ ool | 5. __ ot | 6. __ ad |
| __ ool | __ ot | __ ad |
| __ ool | __ ot | __ ad |
| __ ool | __ ot | __ ad |

ISBN: 978-1-897457-01-6

## 9

*A sentence sometimes tells about what is happening.*

**C.** Complete the following sentences by telling about something that is happening.

**Example:** Amanda is ___playing with her dog___ .

1. David is _____ .

2. Rob is _____ .

3. Maria is _____ .

4. Jim is _____ .

5. Peter and Sam are _____

_____ .

6. Murray and Murphy are _____

_____ .

ISBN: 978-1-897457-01-6

**D.** Read the clues and complete the Opposite Crossword Puzzle with the correct opposite words.

# Opposite Crossword Puzzle

### Across

A. opposite of "inside"
B. opposite of "above"
C. opposite of "up"
D. opposite of "in"

### Down

1. opposite of "under"
2. opposite of "narrow"
3. opposite of "yes"
4. opposite of "from"

# 10 The Yellow Duck

**A. Complete the words in the story.**

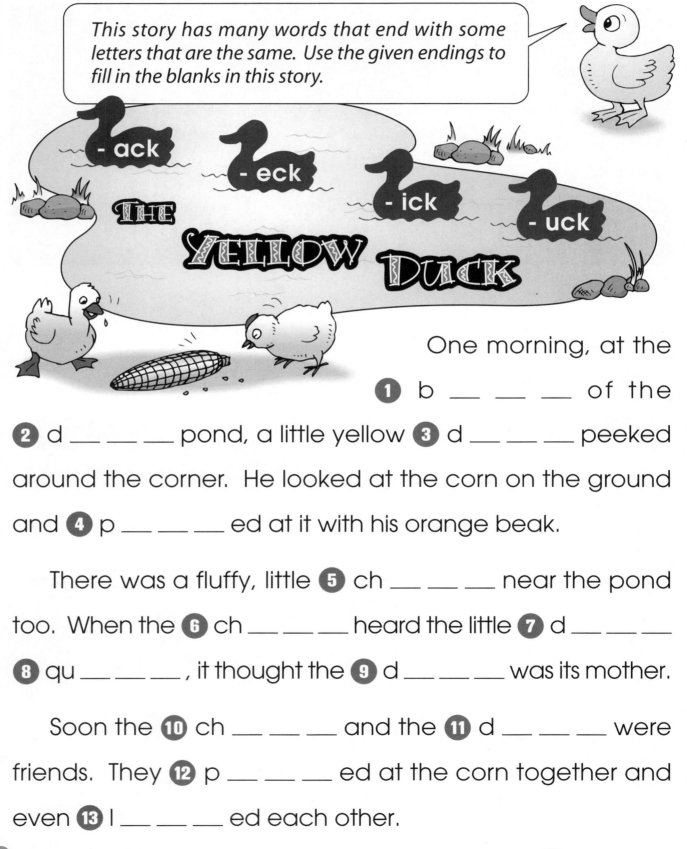

*This story has many words that end with some letters that are the same. Use the given endings to fill in the blanks in this story.*

- ack
- eck
- ick
- uck

One morning, at the ① b __ __ __ of the ② d __ __ __ pond, a little yellow ③ d __ __ __ peeked around the corner. He looked at the corn on the ground and ④ p __ __ __ ed at it with his orange beak.

There was a fluffy, little ⑤ ch __ __ __ near the pond too. When the ⑥ ch __ __ __ heard the little ⑦ d __ __ __ ⑧ qu __ __ __ , it thought the ⑨ d __ __ __ was its mother.

Soon the ⑩ ch __ __ __ and the ⑪ d __ __ __ were friends. They ⑫ p __ __ __ ed at the corn together and even ⑬ l __ __ __ ed each other.

ISBN: 978-1-897457-01-6

## More "ck" Words

**B.** Read the clues and complete the "ck" Crossword Puzzle with words that have "ack", "ick", "ock", or "uck" in them.  Use the Word Bank to help you.

# "ck" Crossword Puzzle

**Across**

A.  A short coat

B.  It tells the time.

C.  There are two of them in your pants.

**Down**

1.  You are ___ when you win.

2.  You buy one to win.

3.  You ___ a soccer ball.

## Word Bank

lucky    pockets    clock    jacket    kick    ticket

ISBN: 978-1-897457-01-6

## 10

Can you think of even more "ck" words?

**C. Use consonants to make new words ending in "ck".**

**Examples:** b̲ack h̲ack

**1. back**

___ ack

___ ack

___ ack

___ ack

___ ack

___ ack

**2. beck**

___ eck

___ eck

**3. kick**

___ ick

___ ick

___ ick

___ ick

___ ick

___ ick

**4. dock**

___ ock

___ ock

___ ock

___ ock

___ ock

**5. duck**

___ uck

___ uck

___ uck

___ uck

___ uck

ISBN: 978-1-897457-01-6

D. **Each of the sentences below has a jumbled "ck" word in the grey box. Write the correctly spelled word on the line. Use the Word Bank to help you.**

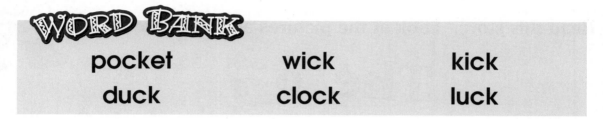

**WORD BANK**

| pocket | wick | kick |
|--------|------|------|
| duck | clock | luck |

1. The time on the ⬛ k c c l o ⬛ read 2:30.

   _____

2. The ⬛ k d c u ⬛ swam in the pond.

   _____

3. The candle ⬛ k c w i ⬛ was long.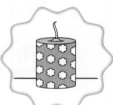

   _____

4. A horseshoe means good ⬛ c l u k ⬛ .

   _____

5. Amanda gave the ball a ⬛ k k c i ⬛ .

   _____

6. Sandra dug in her ⬛ k p o t c e ⬛ for a dime.

   _____

*In a **rebus** story, a picture takes the place of a word.*

**A.  Read this story.  Look at the pictures and fill in the words.**

## The ❶

On Sunday, we made a ❷ .  We rolled some

❸ into a ❹ and kept rolling it until it got bigger

and bigger.  Then, we rolled ❺ **2** more ❻ of

❼ .

We put ❽ **1** ❾ on top of the other until

the ❿ **3** ⓫ were on top of each other.

Finally, we put a ⓬ and a ⓭ on

the ⓮ .  We also used a ⓯ for the nose.

1. _____   2. _____   3. _____

4. _____   5. _____   6. _____

7. _____   8. _____   9. _____

10. _____  11. _____  12. _____

13. _____  14. _____  15. _____

**B.** Each of these words is a winter word. Look at the pictures. Fill in the missing letters.

1. s __ o __

2. s __ o __ m __ n

3. s __ o __ f __ a __ e

4. s __ o __ b __ l __

5. s __ o __ p __ o __

6. s __ a __ f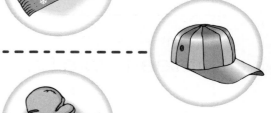

7. c __ p

8. m __ t __ e __ s

9. s __ a __ e __

10. c __ l __

11. i __ e

12. t __ b __ g __ a __

ISBN: 978-1-897457-01-6

**C.** The letters of some words are mixed up in the sentences below. Write the correctly spelled words on the lines.

1. Daniel played in the ⬚ o w n s ⬚ all day.

   _____

2. Andrew made a ⬚ n w m n a s o ⬚ with his mom.

   _____

3. Mom said, "Wear your ⬚ p a c ⬚ and ⬚ t t i m n e s ⬚."

   _____   _____

4. I took my ⬚ b o g t g n a o ⬚ with me.

   _____

5. Kathleen wore her ⬚ k t s a e s ⬚ to the arena.

   _____

6. Our snowman has a striped ⬚ c r f s a ⬚.

   _____

7. "Brrr... it is so ⬚ l d o c ⬚ !"

   _____

8. Gary threw a ⬚ n s w b l l a o ⬚ at his brother.

   _____

**D. Match each word with its meaning. Write the letter in the box.**

1 snowplow

2 toboggan

3 scarf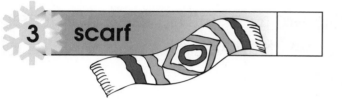

4 mittens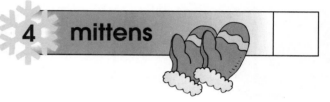

5 cap

6 snowball

7 skates

8 ice

**A** You wear them to slide on ice.

**B** You wear it to keep your head warm.

**C** Water becomes this when it freezes.

**D** It is round and made with snow.

**E** It is the thing you sit on to slide down a hill.

**F** You wear them on your hands in winter.

**G** It is the vehicle that clears the snow on your street.

**H** It is what you wear around your neck to keep it warm.

ISBN: 978-1-897457-01-6

# 12 The Doctor's Tools

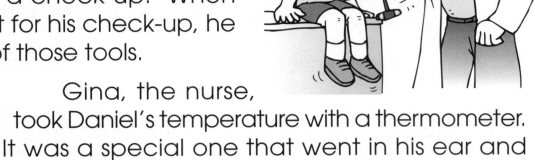

Doctors have "tools" that they use to give a check-up. When Daniel went for his check-up, he saw some of those tools.

Gina, the nurse, took Daniel's temperature with a thermometer. It was a special one that went in his ear and beeped when it was ready.

Dr. Conn used a funny little tool called a "reflex hammer" on Daniel's knees.

Daniel had fun learning about a doctor's tools at his check-up.

**A. Read the passage and put these sentences in the correct order.**

The nurse took his temperature with a thermometer.
Daniel went for his check-up.
Dr. Conn used a "reflex hammer" on his knees.
Doctors have "tools" that they use.

1. _____

2. _____

3. _____

4. _____

ISBN: 978-1-897457-01-6

**B.** **Fill in the blanks with words from the passage.**

1. You go to the _____ when you are sick.

2. We put _____ in a tool box.

3. We use a _____ with nails.

4. Ben's mom took his temperature with a _____ .

5. A _____ helps a doctor in a clinic.

6. Our dog is _____ . It always makes us laugh.

7. It's hot when the _____ is high.

8. We had _____ learning about animals in the zoo.

ISBN: 978-1-897457-01-6

## 12

**C. Complete the sentences below.**

*Don't forget to end a sentence with a period.*

1. The nurse _____

2. A doctor is _____

3. A thermometer is _____

4. One of the doctor's tools is _____

    _____

5. A check-up is _____

6. Dr. Conn checked Daniel's knees with _____

    _____

7. My doctor _____

8. There are a lot of tools _____

    _____

9. The story "The Doctor's Tools" is about _____

    _____

ISBN: 978-1-897457-01-6

**D. There are many kinds of tools. Draw a line to match the name of each tool with the meaning.**

**Example:**

hammer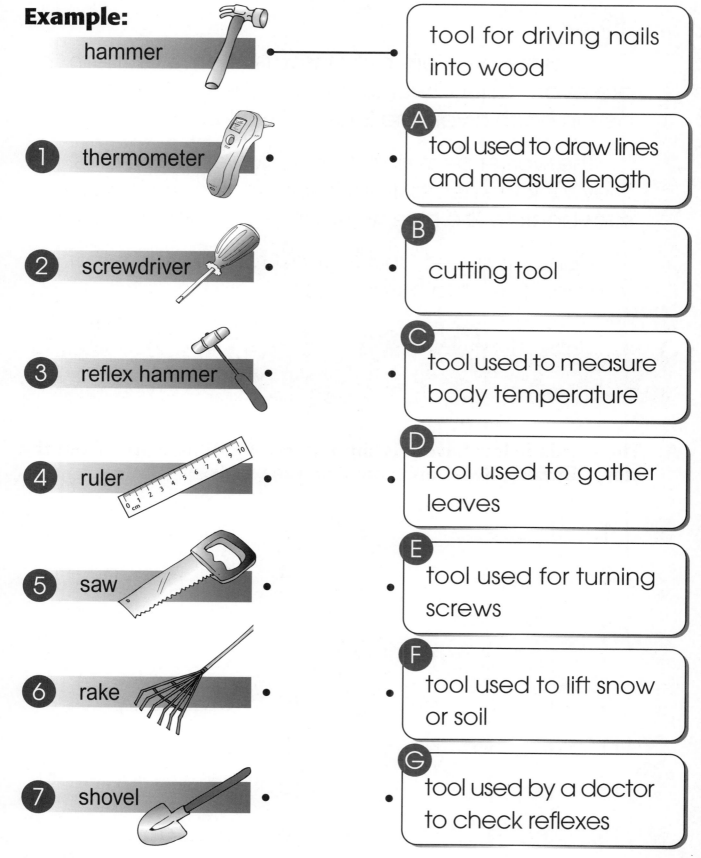

tool for driving nails into wood

1. thermometer

A. tool used to draw lines and measure length

2. screwdriver

B. cutting tool

3. reflex hammer

C. tool used to measure body temperature

4. ruler

D. tool used to gather leaves

5. saw

E. tool used for turning screws

6. rake

F. tool used to lift snow or soil

7. shovel

G. tool used by a doctor to check reflexes

ISBN: 978-1-897457-01-6

# 13 Buzzing Bees

Bees are very busy insects.  Some of them are even called "worker bees".  There is a queen bee in each hive.  She is not a "worker bee".

The worker bees buzz around flowers and plants.  They suck the nectar from them.  They carry food in sacs back to the hive where it is made into honey.

Honey is sweet and is good for you.  That is, if you don't eat too much of it!

**A.** **The words below have missing letters.  Find the words from the story "Buzzing Bees" and complete the words.**

 1.  b __ s __

2.  in __ e __ t __

 3.  w __ rk __ r

4.  q __ e __ n

5.  bu __ __

6.  f __ ow __ r __

 7.  p __ a __ ts

8.  s __ c __

 9.  n __ c __ ar

10.  c __ r __ y

11.  f __ od

12.  s __ __ s

 13.  h __ v __

14.  h __ n __ y

 15.  s __ e __ t

16.  g __ o __

ISBN: 978-1-897457-01-6

**B. Match the two parts of a sentence. Write the letter in the flower.**

(A) is not a worker bee.    (B) busy insects.

(C) sweet.    (D) from flowers.

(E) buzz around flowers.    (F) the hive.

(G) in sacs.    (H) honey from nectar.

1. Bees are · · · · · · · · · · · · · · · · · · · · · · · · · · · · · · · · · · · · · · · · ·

2. The worker bees · · · · · · · · · · · · · · · · · · · · · · · · · · · · · ·

3. The queen bee · · · · · · · · · · · · · · · · · · · · · · · · · · · · · · · ·

4. Bees get nectar · · · · · · · · · · · · · · · · · · · · · · · · · · · · · · ·

5. They make · · · · · · · · · · · · · · · · · · · · · · · · · · · · · · · · · · · · · ·

6. Bees carry food · · · · · · · · · · · · · · · · · · · · · · · · · · · · · · ·

7. Honey is · · · · · · · · · · · · · · · · · · · · · · · · · · · · · · · · · · · · · · · · ·

8. Bees make honey in · · · · · · · · · · · · · · · · · · · · · · · · · · ·

ISBN: 978-1-897457-01-6

## 13

**C.** **Match each word in the Word Bank with its meaning. Write the word in the box.**

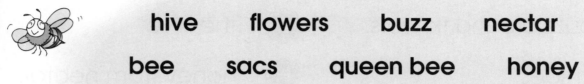

Word Bank

| hive | flowers | buzz | nectar |
| bee | sacs | queen bee | honey |

1. [          ] The sound bees make

2. [          ] Bees carry food in ___ .

3. [          ] The bee in charge

4. [          ] Plants that bees get nectar from

5. [          ] What bees suck from flowers

6. [          ] Where bees make honey

7. [          ] An insect that makes honey

8. [          ] Sweet sticky food bees make

ISBN: 978-1-897457-01-6

## D. Circle the words in the Beehive Word Search.

# Beehive Word Search

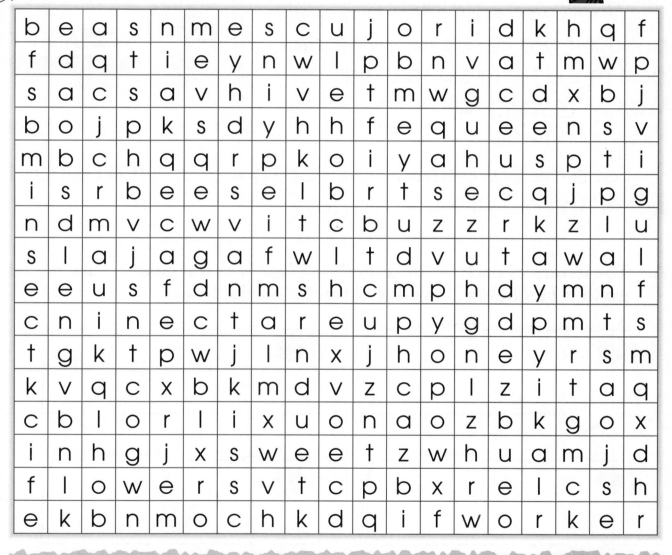

| b | e | a | s | n | m | e | s | c | u | j | o | r | i | d | k | h | q | f |
| f | d | q | t | i | e | y | n | w | l | p | b | n | v | a | t | m | w | p |
| s | a | c | s | a | v | h | i | v | e | t | m | w | g | c | d | x | b | j |
| b | o | j | p | k | s | d | y | h | h | f | e | q | u | e | e | n | s | v |
| m | b | c | h | q | q | r | p | k | o | i | y | a | h | u | s | p | t | i |
| i | s | r | b | e | e | s | e | l | b | r | t | s | e | c | q | j | p | g |
| n | d | m | v | c | w | v | i | t | c | b | u | z | z | r | k | z | l | u |
| s | l | a | j | a | g | a | f | w | l | t | d | v | u | t | a | w | a | l |
| e | e | u | s | f | d | n | m | s | h | c | m | p | h | d | y | m | n | f |
| c | n | i | n | e | c | t | a | r | e | u | p | y | g | d | p | m | t | s |
| t | g | k | t | p | w | j | l | n | x | j | h | o | n | e | y | r | s | m |
| k | v | q | c | x | b | k | m | d | v | z | c | p | l | z | i | t | a | q |
| c | b | l | o | r | l | i | x | u | o | n | a | o | z | b | k | g | o | x |
| i | n | h | g | j | x | s | w | e | e | t | z | w | h | u | a | m | j | d |
| f | l | o | w | e | r | s | v | t | c | p | b | x | r | e | l | c | s | h |
| e | k | b | n | m | o | c | h | k | d | q | i | f | w | o | r | k | e | r |

**flowers     insect     honey     sacs     sweet     queen**
**hive     bees     nectar     buzz     worker     plants**

On Monday, we went for a bus ride.  First, Mom had to go to a <u>store</u> to get <u>coins</u> so that we had the correct <u>change</u> to give to the bus <u>driver</u>.

When we got on the bus, we put our <u>money</u> in a box.  We rode past many houses and buildings.  We saw <u>flowers</u> in bloom and new leaves on trees.

Soon the bus came to our stop so we rang the bell and got off the bus.  It was a fun day!

**A.** **The letters of each of the underlined words in the passage are mixed up in a bus below.  Spell it correctly on the lines.**

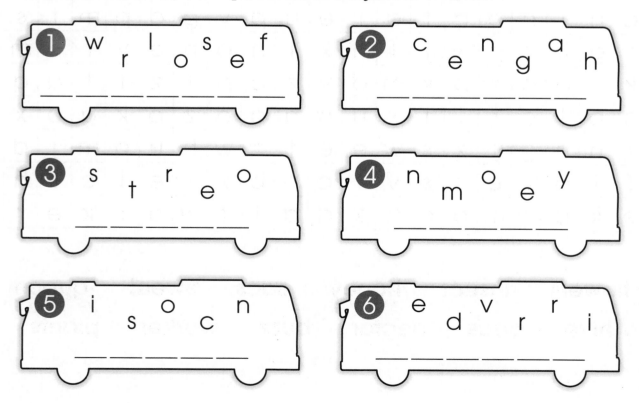

1  w l s f r o e  _____

2  c n a e g h  _____

3  s t r e o  _____

4  n m o e y  _____

5  i o n s c  _____

6  e v r d r i  _____

**B.** **Each of the pictures below tells about a word from "The Bus Ride".**
**Write the word below the picture.**

1.

_____

2.

_____

3.

_____

4.

_____

5.

_____

6.

_____

7.

_____

8.

_____

ISBN: 978-1-897457-01-6

## C. Complete the sentences with the given words.

change    Monday    store    bell
coin    money    flowers

1. A dime is a ten-cent _____ .

2. Please ring the _____ for me.

3. Judy keeps her _____ in a cute piggy bank.

4. They went into the _____ to buy some drinks.

5. _____ is the second day of the week.

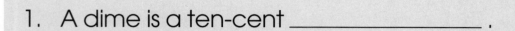

6. Have you got _____ for a five-dollar note?

7. Mom planted the _____ in the backyard.

ISBN: 978-1-897457-01-6

**D. Put the mixed-up words in each group in the correct order to form a sentence. Write it on the lines.**

1. like   rides   .   bus   We   take   to

_____

_____

2. hat   The   wears   bus   a   driver   .

_____

_____

3. rang   bell   We   the   stop   bus   . to   the

_____

_____

4. had   fun   !   We   lots   of

_____

_____

5. you   Do   the   ride   bus   ?

_____

_____

6. ride   I   school   bus   .   a   on

_____

I have a monster that lives in my closet. It is not a scary monster. It is a friendly monster.

My monster has two big, green eyes, pink fur, and three fingers on each hand. It has four toes on each foot and five teeth in its mouth.

At night, when I go to bed, my monster takes care of me. No scary monsters come around when my favourite monster is there.

**A. Find number words and words that name body parts in the passage and write them in the correct boxes.**

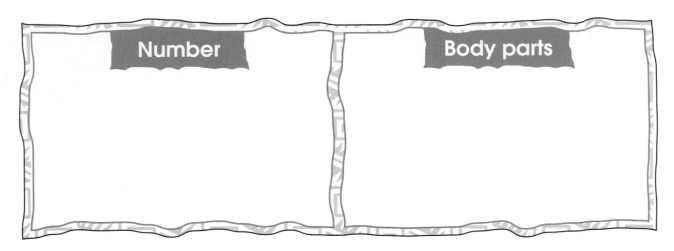

| Number | Body parts |
| --- | --- |
|  |  |

**B. Each of the phrases (groups of words) below is from "My Favourite Monster". Draw a picture to go with each phrase.**

1.

a scary monster

2.

a friendly monster

3.

two big, green eyes

4.

three fingers
on each hand

5.

four toes on each foot

6.

five teeth in its mouth

**C.** **Each monster below has a word from "My Favourite Monster".
Unscramble the word and write it on the line.**

**D.** Jenny is looking for her favourite monster. Fill in the missing letters in each word. Use the word bank to help you.

bed   fur   monster   two   lives   three   pink
closet   scary   green   fingers   big   friendly
toes   teeth   foot   five   go   night   four

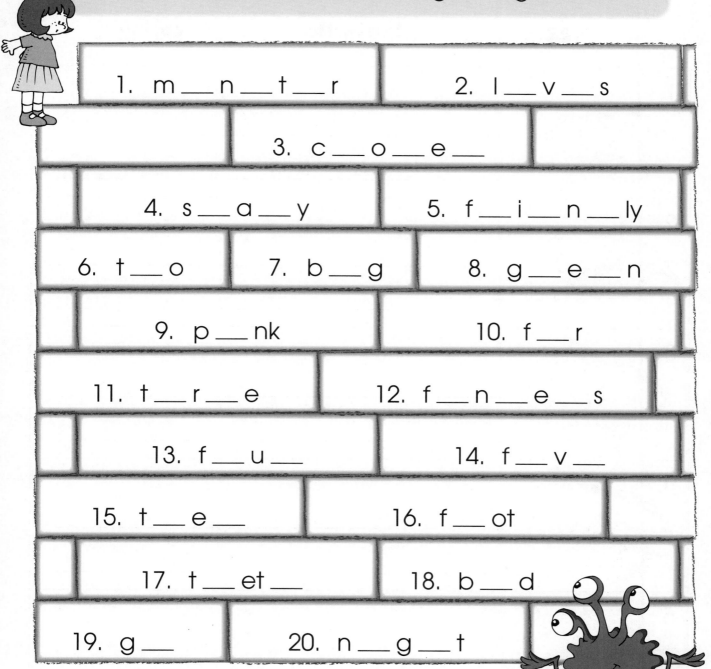

1. m __ n __ t __ r

2. l __ v __ s

3. c __ o __ e __

4. s __ a __ y

5. f __ i __ n __ ly

6. t __ o

7. b __ g

8. g __ e __ n

9. p __ nk

10. f __ r

11. t __ r __ e

12. f __ n __ e __ s

13. f __ u __

14. f __ v __

15. t __ e __

16. f __ ot

17. t __ et __

18. b __ d

19. g __

20. n __ g __ t

ISBN: 978-1-897457-01-6

**A.** The story below is in pictures. Write a sentence that goes with each picture to tell the story. Use the given words to help you.

cocoon          leaf          caterpillar

egg          butterfly          eating

| | |
|---|---|
| 1. | _____ <br> _____ |
| 2. | _____ <br> _____ |
| 3. | _____ <br> _____ |
| 4. | _____ <br> _____ |
| 5. | _____ <br> _____ |

ISBN: 978-1-897457-01-6

**B.** The story below has some pictures that take the place of words. Fill in the words.

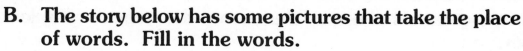

My  1._____ just got a new pet

2._____ . We went to the pet  3._____ .

The  4._____ at the  5._____ told

us that  6._____ make very good pets.

We also saw  7._____ ,  8._____ ,

 9._____ , and  10._____ at the pet

 11._____ . I would really ♡ 12._____ to

get a  13._____ , but  14._____ says

15._____ need lots of  16._____ .

**C.** **Read each of the clues. Find a word that means the same to complete the crossword puzzle.**

Across

A. repair

B. all by itself

C. right

D. 365 days

Down

1. put in

2. good

3. unusual

4. neat

5. mom

ISBN: 978-1-897457-01-6

**D.**

**F. Put the mixed-up words in the correct order to form a sentence.
Write it on the line.**

1. winter   .   We   to   like   in   skate

_____

2. Ron   bus   is   driver   .   a

_____

3. Kathy   read   books   .   to   loves

_____

4. swims   Mandy   the   pool   in   house
   her   .   at

_____

5. cook   ?   like   Do   to   you

_____

6. blue   .   new   My   coat   is

_____

ISBN: 978-1-897457-01-6

ISBN: 978-1-897457-01-6

# 1 Follow the small letters in abc order to find out what treat Little Jerry can get.

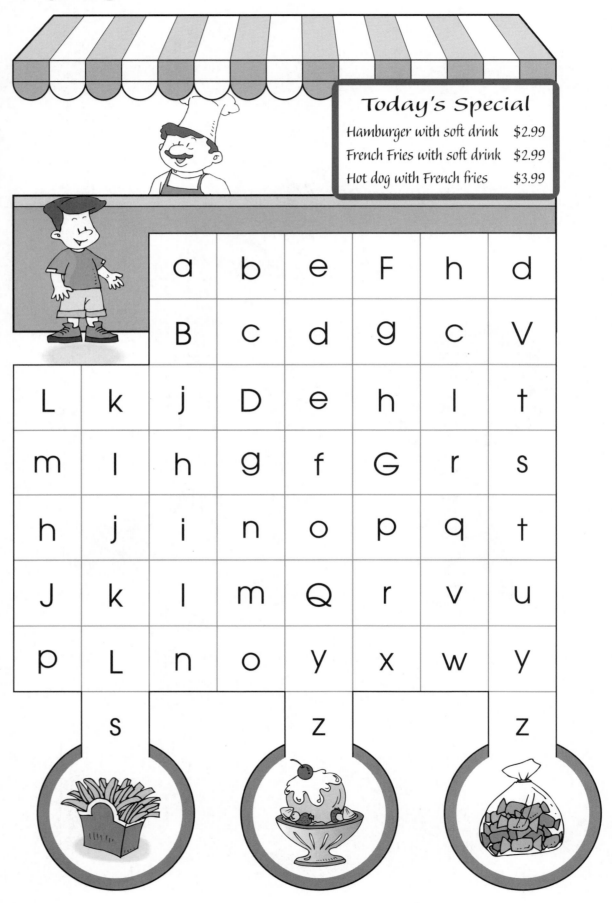

| a | b | e | F | h | d |
|---|---|---|---|---|---|
| B | c | d | g | c | V |
| L | k | j | D | e | h | l | t |
| m | l | h | g | f | G | r | s |
| h | j | i | n | o | p | q | t |
| J | k | l | m | Q | r | v | u |
| p | L | n | o | y | x | w | y |

s      z      z

**2** What makes Little Shark so scared? Connect the dots from a to z to find out what it is.

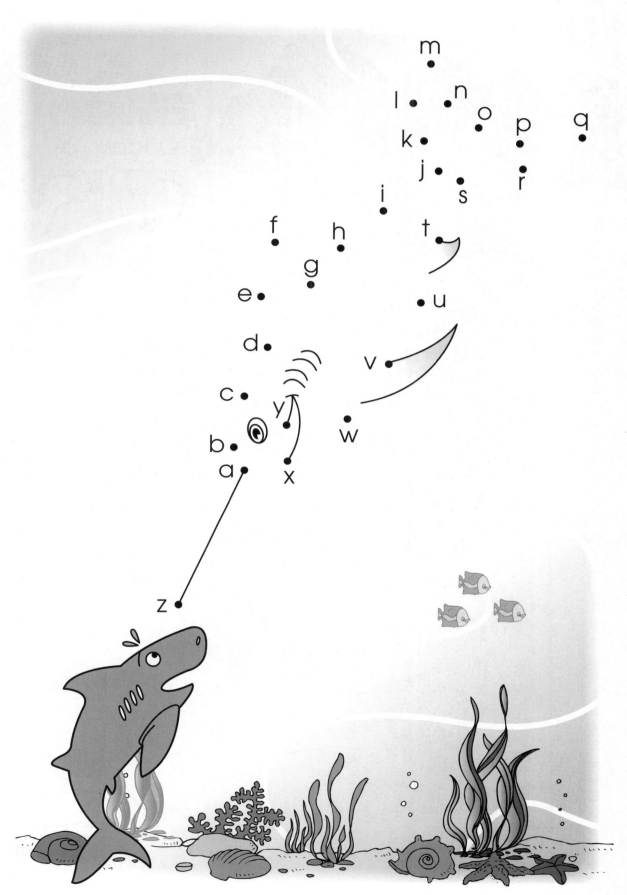

# 3

**Only the ducklings with vowels are Mother Duck's babies. Colour them.**

ISBN: 978-1-897457-01-6

**4** Draw the cover of the storybook.

The Fairy's Pet

**5** Cross out letters in alphabetical order from A to Z to find out what Mother Bear says. The first three have been done for you.

~~A~~ W E ~~B~~ R A R E L Y ~~C~~ D E
S E E F G H O T H E R I J
P O L A R K B E A R S L M
N O O N P T H I S Q R S T
B A R E U L A N D V W O F
X Y Z S N O W .

A B C W E D E D O F G H I
J N O T K F I N D L A N Y
M N P E N G U I N S O P Q
R S T U H E R E V W X Y Z
E I T H E R .

ISBN: 978-1-897457-01-6

# 6

**Circle the pets in the Pet Word Search.**

## Pet Word Search

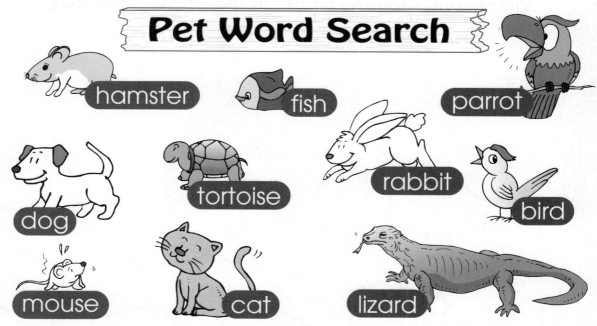

hamster

fish

parrot

dog

tortoise

rabbit

bird

mouse

cat

lizard

| e | k | r | q | d | c | j | b | o | m | q | h |
|---|---|---|---|---|---|---|---|---|---|---|---|
| j | a | n | f | t | v | n | s | d | o | g | i |
| u | c | a | t | y | g | w | f | r | u | d | l |
| p | h | l | m | u | m | a | v | p | s | e | p |
| s | x | g | f | o | z | i | t | s | e | c | a |
| f | c | l | i | b | l | h | o | g | k | j | r |
| v | d | i | s | e | x | r | r | d | n | t | r |
| i | o | z | h | a | j | a | t | s | z | b | o |
| l | w | a | x | m | u | b | o | y | f | q | t |
| b | i | r | d | y | e | b | i | p | w | h | r |
| m | z | d | k | r | b | i | s | t | o | a | m |
| g | c | h | a | m | s | t | e | r | d | k | i |

**7** Help Wincy the Witch find the castle in the sky. Colour the clouds following the letters in the words "sky castle".

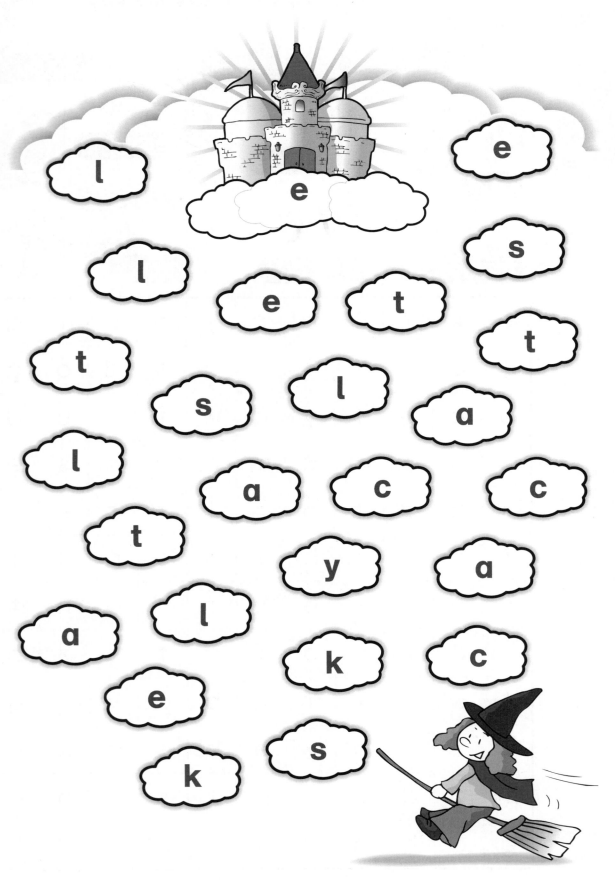

**8** Natalie is having fun on the sea. Colour the spaces to find out where she is.

**sh-words** – purple
**long i** – black
**short u** – blue
**short e** – white
**others** – green

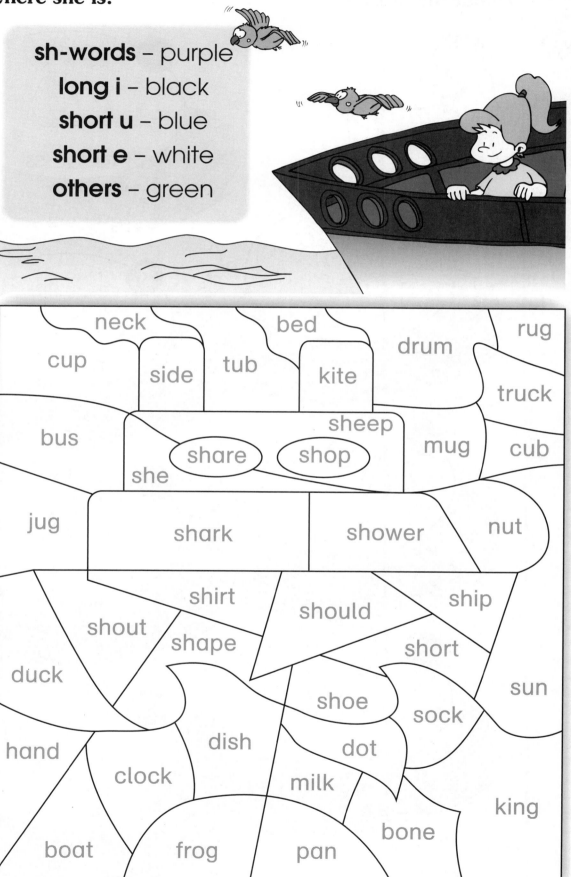

neck    bed    rug
cup    side    tub    kite    drum
truck
bus    sheep    mug    cub
share    shop
she
jug    shark    shower    nut
shirt    should    ship
shout    shape    short
duck    shoe    sock    sun
hand    dish    dot
clock    milk    king
boat    frog    pan    bone

**9**  Mother Hen has laid some huge eggs.  Complete the words and colour the pictures.

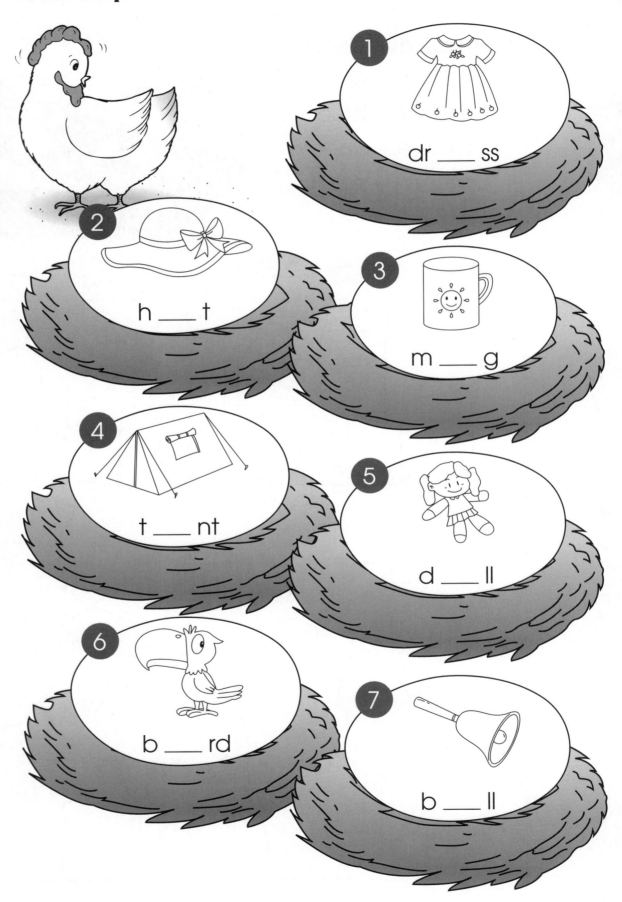

1  dr ___ ss

2  h ___ t

3  m ___ g

4  t ___ nt

5  d ___ ll

6  b ___ rd

7  b ___ ll

  ISBN: 978-1-897457-01-6

Lilian the Ladybug wants to get to the centre of the flower. Colour her path following the letters in the words "little ladybug".

| | l | | l | | i | | t | |
|---|---|---|---|---|---|---|---|---|
| e | | e | | i | | t | | l | e |
| e | | l | t | | t | l | | e | l | e |
| l | | e | e | | t | | l | | l | a | | d |
| a | | l | b | | a | | g | u | | u | b | | y |
| t | | a | d | | y | | b | | g | | u | | y |
| | d | | d | b | | y | | u | | g |
| | | b | | u | | g | | l |

**Read the clues. Complete the Family Crossword Puzzle.**

**Across**

A. Father of your father
B. Boys born to the same mom
C. Your mom's sister
D. Mother of your father

**Down**

1. Children of your mom's sister
2. Your mom's brother
3. Girls born to the same mom
4. Another word for "father"
5. Another word for "mother"

## Family Crossword Puzzle

ISBN: 978-1-897457-01-6

## 12 Name the fruits and vegetables.

pineapple    mushroom    eggplant    mango
watermelon    pear    tomato    carrot

**1** _____

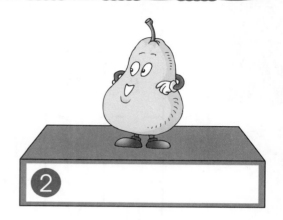

**2** _____

**3** _____

**4** _____

**5** _____

**6** _____

**7** _____

**8** _____

ISBN: 978-1-897457-01-6

# 13

Simon the Snake is going home. Follow the names of the pictures below the maze to find out where Simon lives.

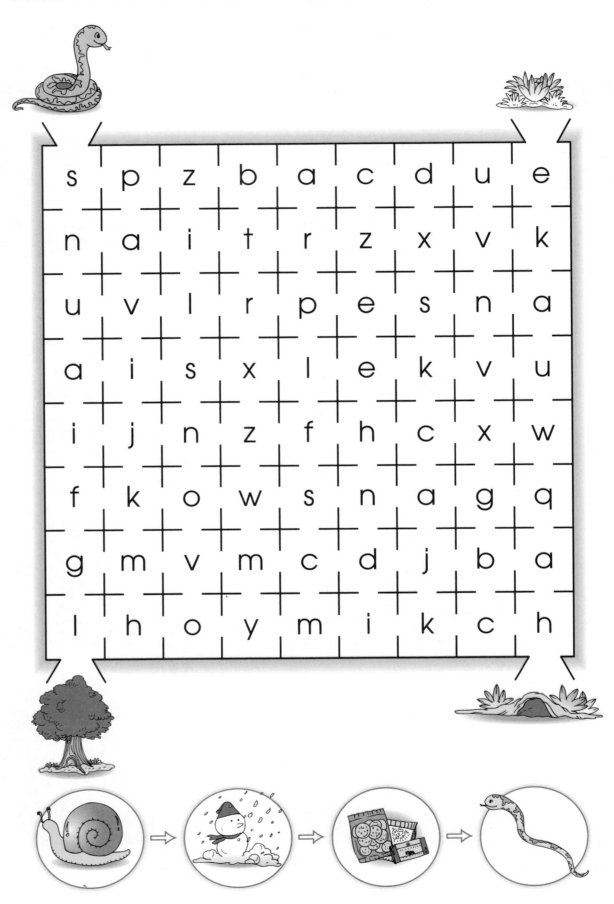

ISBN: 978-1-897457-01-6

## 14

Jenny is trapped in a haunted house. Help her get out by filling in the missing letters for the things she sees.

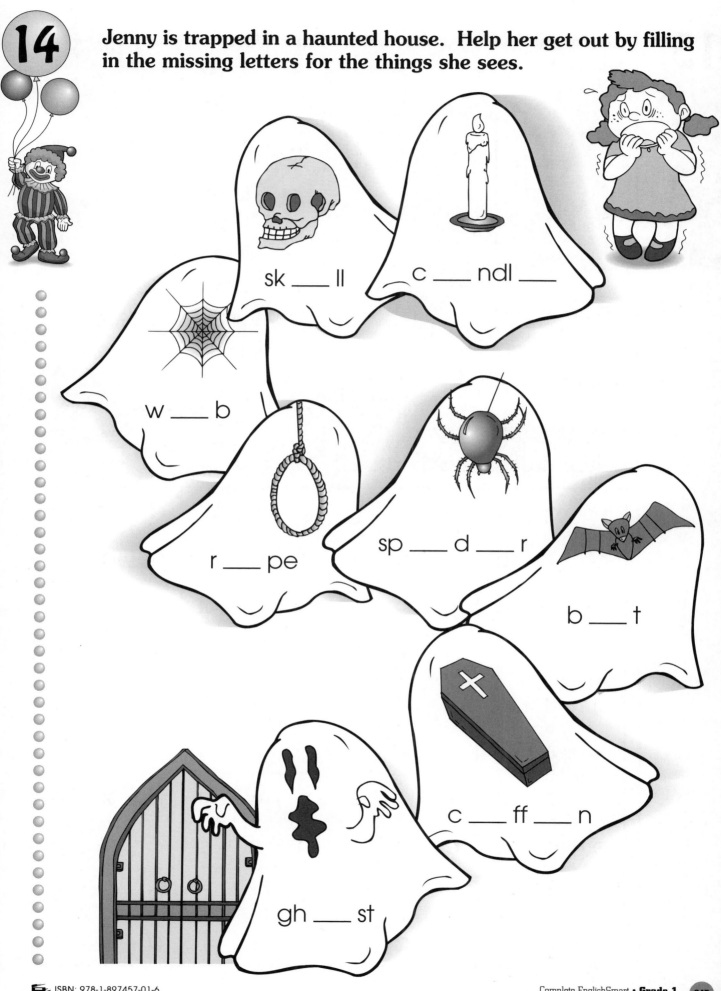

sk ___ ll

c ___ ndl ___

w ___ b

r ___ pe

sp ___ d ___ r

b ___ t

c ___ ff ___ n

gh ___ st

ISBN: 978-1-897457-01-6

# 15

Circle the "park" words in the Park Word Search.

birds    kids
trees    bugs
slide    swings
ducks    pond
squirrels    geese
benches    flowers

PARK WORD SEARCH

| n | q | d | b | j | g | y | k | m | d | l | o |
|---|---|---|---|---|---|---|---|---|---|---|---|
| p | t | c | i | n | x | r | w | b | u | g | s |
| l | r | o | r | p | s | b | u | a | c | p | g |
| s | e | t | d | x | k | m | f | z | k | w | s |
| g | e | e | s | e | i | z | l | e | s | s | w |
| k | s | r | m | w | d | p | o | n | d | v | i |
| t | d | b | i | l | s | b | w | h | p | x | n |
| e | q | b | e | n | c | h | e | s | c | m | g |
| h | l | n | s | q | u | i | r | r | e | l | s |
| b | s | l | i | d | e | g | s | f | a | k | r |

ISBN: 978-1-897457-01-6

# 16

**Read the clues. Complete the crossword puzzle with the colour of each thing.**

## Across

A. a mango
B. a tree trunk
C. grass
D. a grape
E. a night sky

## Down

1. a clear sky
2. a strawberry
3. a peach
4. a papaya
5. a polar bear

**17** Draw lines to join the rhyming pairs.

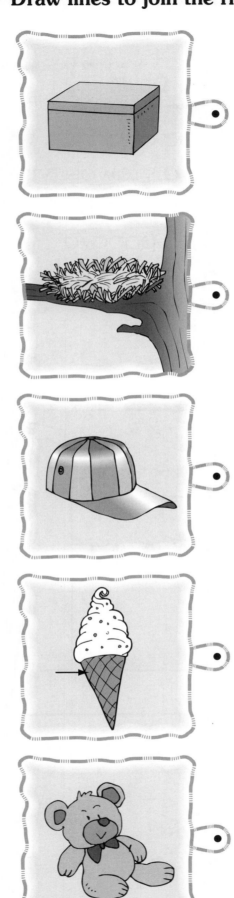

ISBN: 978-1-897457-01-6

**18** Help Little Bee fly to the flowers. Colour the path following the one-syllable words.

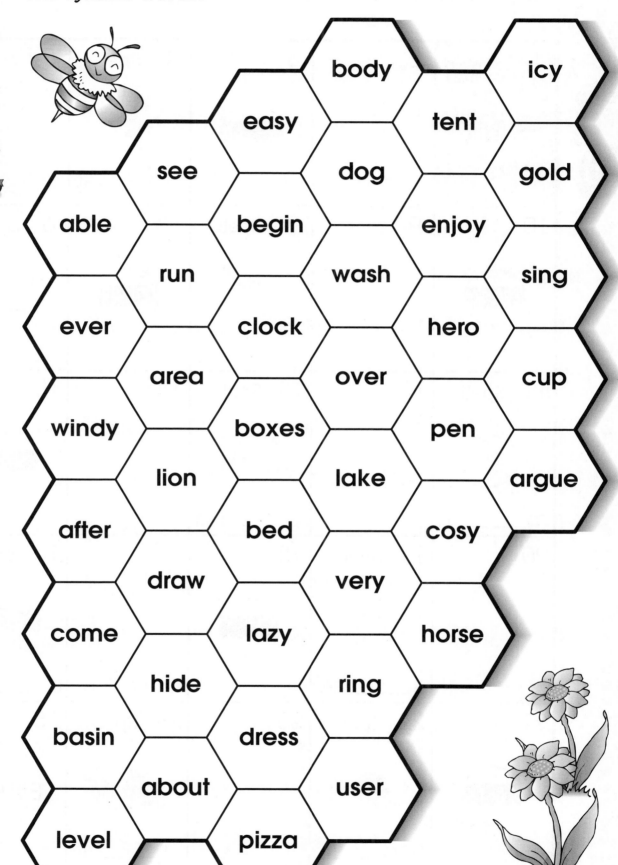

body · icy · easy · tent · see · dog · gold · able · begin · enjoy · run · wash · sing · ever · clock · hero · area · over · cup · windy · boxes · pen · lion · lake · argue · after · bed · cosy · draw · very · come · lazy · horse · hide · ring · basin · dress · about · user · level · pizza

ISBN: 978-1-897457-01-6

**19**

**Stanley and Stella are playing a game called "Stop and Spell".
Help them finish the words.**

| 1 Start | 2 | 3 | 4 Spell <br> __ __ ail | 5 |
|---|---|---|---|---|
| 10 | 9 | 8 Spell <br> be __ __ | 7 | 6 Spell <br> __ __ ck |
| 11 Spell <br> m __ __ n | 12 | 13 Spell <br> __ __ ing | 14 | 15 |
| 20 | 19 Spell <br> s __ __ le | 18 | 17 | 16 Spell <br> c __ __ dy |
| 21 | 22 Spell <br> aco __ __ | 23 | 24 Spell <br> l __ __ f | 25 Finish |

ISBN: 978-1-897457-01-6

**20** Dad has given Mom a ring. Where does Mom put it? Write the names of the things. Change a letter each time. Draw the ring in the last picture.

1. r | | r | n | g

2. | | i | n | g

3. | | i | n | g

4. w | i | n | |

5. w | | n | d

6. | | a | n | d

7. | | a | n | d

ISBN: 978-1-897457-01-6

ISBN: 978-1-897457-01-6

**1  Tom's Toy Train**

A.
1. It was blue.
2. It was about a toy train.
3. The train came to life.
4. He went around the world.

C.

E.

F.
1. Ted has a toy train.
2. He takes it out of the box.
3. He puts it together.
4. He flips the switch.
5. It goes around the track.

G. (Suggested drawing and answer)

doll    ball

H.
1. The <u>boy</u> is looking at the train.
2. The story is about a <u>fireman</u>.
3. An animal <u>doctor</u> helps sick animals.
4. A <u>baker</u> makes cookies and cakes.

**2  Shopping Fun**

A.
1. School is starting soon.
2. They are going to shop today.
3. They are shopping for new clothes for school.
4. They will have lunch at a restaurant.

C.

E.

F.
1. We buy the ingredients.
2. We mix the ingredients.
3. We put the cake in the oven.
4. We spread the icing. Yum! Yum!

G.
1. The whales live in the <u>ocean</u>.
2. Last summer, we went to the <u>zoo</u>.
3. We will go to the <u>store</u> after lunch.
4. The <u>park</u> has swings.
5. We visited a <u>farm</u> on our vacation.
6. Let's go shopping in the new <u>mall</u>.

H. (Suggested drawing)

orange    Draw yourself here.

**3  Muffy the New Dog**

A.
1. dog
2. Muffy
3. fetch
4. carpet

D.
1. m    2. d    3. m    4. d
5. m    6. d    7. d    8. m
9. m    10. d    11. m    12. d

E.
1. The moving truck came to our house.
2. The movers carried everything onto the truck.
3. The moving truck drove away.
4. The house is empty. Goodbye, house!

F.
1. boy       2. girls
3. birds     4. dog
5. tree      6. flowers
7. swing     8. squirrels

**4  The Race**

A.
1. Dan and Fiona ran in the race.
2. They started at the red line beside the fence.
3. Fiona was in the lead at first.
4. Fiona won the race.

C.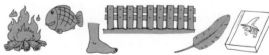

E. (Suggested drawing)

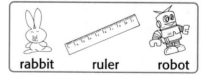

rabbit    ruler    robot

F. (Suggested drawing)

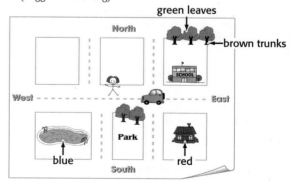

green leaves
North
brown trunks
SCHOOL
West    East
Park
blue    red
South

G.
1. crayons    2. boxes
3. markers    4. blocks
5. dishes     6. rugs

H.
1. fence      2. river / stream
3. fire

## 5 Plants

A. 1. Plants are living things.
2. They make their own food.
3. They need light and water.
4. They get light from the sun.
5. They get water from the rain.

C.
g ___ g ___ ___ g ___ g

E.

F. 1. We buy the seeds.
2. We dig the soil.
3. We plant the seeds.
4. It rains; then the sun shines.
5. The plant sprouts.

G. (Suggested answers)
1. sun               2. rain
3. food              4. water
5. plants

H. 1. We have a pet cat.
2. The apple is tasty.
3. It is sunny outside.
4. There are rows and rows of corn.

## 6 Hens and Chicks

A. 1. He has been learning about chicks and hens.
2. It is a bird.
3. They grow inside eggs.
4. They peck at the shells.

C.

E. 1. n      2. h      3. h      4. h
5. n      6. n      7. h      8. n

F. 1. The hen lays an egg.
2. The hen sits on the egg to warm it.
3. The baby chick pecks at the shell.
4. The chick hatches from the shell.

G. 1. chicken          2. hatch
3. pecks

H. 1. no               2. yes
3. yes               4. no
5. yes

I. (Suggested drawing)

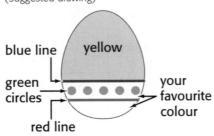
blue line | yellow
green circles
red line
your favourite colour

## 7 Judy the Witch

A. 1. friendly          2. boots
3. watch             4. moon

C.

E.

F. (Suggested drawing and individual colouring)

G. 1. Jim <u>rides</u> his bike.
2. David <u>plays</u> the guitar.
3. Kathleen <u>looks</u> at the stars.
4. Rob <u>works</u> at school.
5. Mary <u>cooks</u> her dinner.
6. Dad <u>baked</u> a cake.
7. They <u>walked</u> to the store.
8. The girls <u>jumped</u> over the rope.
9. Christina <u>skates</u> every week.
10. Ryan <u>likes</u> baseball.

## 8 Flying Kites

A. 1. It is selling kites.
2. They are boxes, diamonds, dragons, and more.
3. The sky is so bright.
4. It is $5.00.
5. It appears three times.

C. (connecting lines image)

E.
| b | d | u | x | c | o | l | v | m | v | r | s | v | a | v | k | m | v | h |
|---|---|---|---|---|---|---|---|---|---|---|---|---|---|---|---|---|---|---|
| q | c | f | h | i | e | v | a | l | e | n | t | i | n | e | g | i | a | k |
| t | v | i | o | l | i | n | w | f | s | v | a | n | z | s | t | u | s | s |
| l | a | i | r | a | i | n | r | r | t | t | b | e | o | f | o | v | e | n |

F. 1. We hang lights around the tree.
2. We put colourful balls on the tree.
3. We put a star at the treetop.
4. We put presents under the tree.
5. We turn on the lights. How beautiful!

ISBN: 978-1-897457-01-6

G.  1.  I          2.  B
    3.  H          4.  G
    5.  D          6.  C
    7.  F          8.  A
    9.  E

## 9  Zoey at the Zoo

A.  1.  Zoey is a zebra.
    2.  He lives at the zoo.
    3.  Lily and Luther are his parents.
    4.  They came to live at the zoo before Zoey was born.
    5.  He likes to lie in the warm sun.

D.

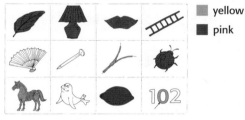

■ yellow
■ pink

E.  1.  First, I colour my picture.
    2.  Next, I glue my picture to the construction paper.
    3.  Then, I cut out my picture.
    4.  Finally, I hang my picture on the wall.

F.  (Suggested drawing)

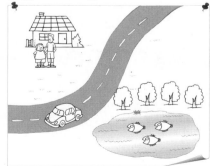

G.  (Suggested answers)
    1.  zoo    2.  sand    3.  bad     4.  feed
    5.  we     6.  tag     7.  honey   8.  mouse
    9.  free   10. can

H.  1.  A          2.  T
    3.  A          4.  T
    5.  T

## Progress Test 1

A.  1.  We asked our mom for an old blanket.
    2.  We got some clothespins.
    3.  We took everything out to the backyard.
    4.  We pinned the blanket to the clothesline.
    5.  We are cozy inside our tent.

B.  1.  d     2.  t     3.  l     4.  s
    5.  b     6.  m     7.  f     8.  r
    9.  g     10. J     11. w     12. p
    13. h     14. n     15. k

C.  (Suggested drawing)

E.  1.  a bee         2.  cups
    3.  cats          4.  socks
    5.  an egg        6.  chicks

F.  1.  dolls         2.  clock
    3.  school        4.  apple
    5.  toys          6.  cars

G.  1.  Pat went to the zoo.
    2.  They had fun at the park.
    3.  Will you go to the store?
    4.  How do you go to school?
    5.  When are you coming to my house?
    6.  There are some rabbits on the grass.

## 10  The Fox and the Queen

A.  1.  queen         2.  fox
    3.  wood          4.  questioned
    5.  queen         6.  palace
    7.  questions     8.  cunning
    9.  palace        10. slept
    11. box           12. jewels

D.

■ green
■ red

E.  1.  Buy the sticks, paper, glue, and string.
    2.  Cut the paper, string, and sticks.
    3.  Glue the sticks and string to the paper.
    4.  Fly the kite.

F.  1.  playing       2.  dancers
    3.  talks         4.  name
    5.  baking        6.  went
    7.  run           8.  barked

## 11  The Wild Yak

A.  1.  It is a large ox.
    2.  It lives in Tibet.
    3.  It eats grass.
    4.  Its hair is black.
    5.  They are 1.8 metres tall.

ISBN: 978-1-897457-01-6

C.

D.
1. Put on a helmet first.
2. Put one leg over the top of the bike to sit down.
3. Next, place your feet on the pedals.
4. Away you go!

E.
1. Where
2. Who
3. When
4. What
5. Why
6. How

F. (Individual colouring and drawing)

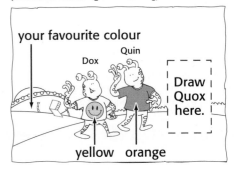

## 12 The Tree House

A.
1. His name is Robert.
2. He built a tree house with his father.
3. They used some wood and nails to build it.
4. They built it in the big tree in their backyard.
5. They built it in the summer.

B.
1. e
2. o
3. i
4. e
5. i
6. u
7. a
8. o
9. u ; e ; a

C.
1. I have a yo-yo.
2. I wind the string around my yo-yo.
3. I let the yo-yo fall.
4. My yo-yo goes up and down.

D.
1. A wild yak has long horns.
2. You have a pretty smile.
3. I need a yellow crayon.
4. The bird sings in a cage.
5. I like to play with my dog.
6. Look at my cute dog.
7. They are yummy bananas.

## 13 Bart the Bear

A.
1. bear
2. winter
3. hungry
4. roots and berries
5. Honey
6. Canada

B.
1. d
2. t
3. d
4. t
5. b
6. d
7. b
8. t
9. t

C. (Suggested drawing)

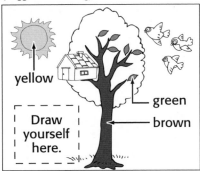

D.
1. There are many bluebirds in the sky.
2. Where are my skates?
3. The flowers are in bloom.

E.
1. under
2. above
3. large
4. tiny

## 14 Making Blueberry Jam

A.
1. The first thing is to pick blueberries.
2. They go to their secret place.
3. They clean the berries and take out the leaves.

B.

C. (Individual writing)

D.

| | | | | | | |
|B| |A C A R R O T| | | | |
|A| | A | A | | |
|B T E N T| |C K I T E| |
| | | E | |

E.
1. played
2. is
3. gave
4. will
5. had
6. rained
7. won
8. wanted

## 15 Pretty Lights

A.
1. It is about pretty lights.
2. The writer is talking about night time.
3. They are in the city.
4. (Individual answers)

B.

C.

| B | L | N | P | E | C | A | S | T | L | E | E | S |
|---|---|---|---|---|---|---|---|---|---|---|---|---|
| N | R | R | A | K | V | O | M | U | K | X | N | N |
| G | F | O | C | H | I | L | D | R | E | N | T | Y |
| J | U | X | O | M | J | D | E | T | A | U | R | B |
| S | T | M | I | R | O | T | W | L | I | G | H | T |
| U | J | F | N | E | C | H | J | E | O | C | L | V |
| B | S | J | Y | F | L | C | N | S | E | V | O | I |
| K | T | A | V | C | N | E | D | B | G | H | P | S |
| T | O | M | O | R | R | O | W | S | C | L | O | D |
| O | P | B | C | A | C | L | E | V | Y | E | G | E |
| D | R | L | H | G | O | C | A | C | B | A | T | R |
| A | U | I | V | D | J | H | F | R | A | F | S | M |
| Y | N | C | S | C | H | O | O | L | U | E | B | I |
| V | B | A | F | J | S | P | L | D | T | S | U | A |

D.
1. night     2. soft
3. go     4. black
5. yes     6. sad
7. little     8. awake

## 16   What Am I?

A.
1. a drum     2. the sun
3. a ball     4. a coin
5. a book

B.

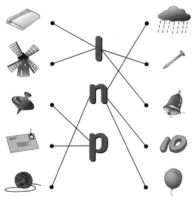

C. (Individual drawings and answer)
D.
1. mug     2. so
3. run     4. bag
5. bed     6. pot
7. it     8. hook
9. bake

## 17   Fun at School

A.
1. She is talking about her school.
2. She plays games to learn new words.
3. She counts teddy bear cookies.
4. She likes her school.

B.
1. c ; p     2. h ; t
3. b ; d     4. t ; p
5. b ; l     6. t ; t
7. j ; m     8. b ; g
9. b ; d     10. d ; r
11. p ; n     12. c ; t

C.

| G | A | B | F | H | B | K | S | N | O | B | M | W |
|---|---|---|---|---|---|---|---|---|---|---|---|---|
| U | T | N | G | D | O | L | L | T | N | A | C | F |
| D | B | L | H | O | X | A | B | I | R | D | C | M |
| U | E | O | T | O | U | F | C | U | P | Q | J | Q |
| V | R | F | U | R | L | P | Q | D | V | W | V | F |
| X | Y | B | H | T | C | A | P | R | J | B | A | G |
| T | N | G | D | H | U | N | Q | U | X | V | N |
| R | O | Y | X | A | M | P | C | M | O | B | H | B |
| S | T | E | N | T | J | Y | N | X | I | T | R | E |
| E | K | V | R | N | W | B | A | L | L | G | D | D |
| O | L | X | S | U | F | C | P | E | F | W | O | X |
| T | O | P | C | A | T | I | G | H | G | T | G | A |

D. (Suggested answers)
1. bat ; fat ; mat     2. bib ; nib ; rib
3. bad ; dad ; mad     4. fit ; hit ; kit
5. gap ; lap ; map     6. bid ; did ; kid

## 18   Sweet Maple Syrup

A.
1. Sugar Bush     2. maple
3. buckets     4. syrup

B.

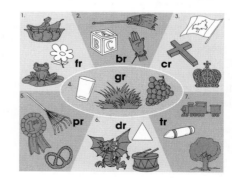

C.

D. (Suggested answers)
1. br
2. cr
3. gr
4. cr
5. gr
6. dr
7. fr
8. tr
9. pr
10. cr

E.
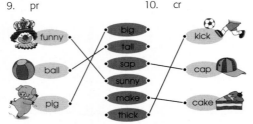

F. 1. My name is Jenny.
2. The cat is sleeping.
3. Go Leafs go!
4. Pat has one brother and one sister.

G.

| small | tiny | up | down | | |
|---|---|---|---|---|---|
| ★ | ○ | ☆ | ● | | |
| big | large | below | under | happy | sad |
| ★ | ○ | ★ | ○ | ☆ | ● |
| stop | go | big | little | yes | no |
| ☆ | ● | ☆ | ● | ☆ | ● |

H. 1. duck
2. made
3. to
4. pull
5. fully

## Progress Test 2

A. 1. His favourite hobby is collecting rocks.
2. He goes for long walks with his mom.
3. He collects the rocks from summer to fall.
4. They find the rocks on the sides of the roads and on paths.
5. Some rocks have spots, some have stripes, and others have many colours.
6. He has more than a hundred rocks in his collection.

B. 1. a
2. i
3. e
4. a
5. u
6. e
7. i
8. o
9. u
10. o
11. e
12. i

C. 1. q
2. x
3. y
4. q
5. n
6. t
7. p
8. k

D.
1. hat — something to wear on your head
2. cat — an animal with whiskers and a long tail
3. bat — a flying mammal
4. man — an adult human male
5. fan — It keeps you cool in summer.
6. can — made of a metal, like tin
7. van — It carries a lot of people.
8. pan — something to cook in
9. fin — A fish has one.

E. 1. A rainbow
2. The sun

F. 1. Go to the cupboard .
2. Take out a cone.
3. Take the ice cream out of the freezer.
4. Use a scoop to pick up the ice cream.
5. Put some sprinkles on top.
6. (Individual writing)

## 1 Nouns (1)

A. Place: school ; beach
Thing: mitten ; jam
Person: mother ; nurse
Animal: rabbit ; moose

B. (Colour these words.)
carrot ; star ; boat ; table ; water ; worker ; grass ; singer ;
song ; bag

C. 1. boy
2. girl ; apple
3. cat ; milk
4. dog ; table
5. baby
6. fish ; river
7. mall ; house
8. storybook

D. Common Noun: car ; school ; mouse
Proper Noun: Barbie ; Ottawa ; Kim

E. 1. December ; Christmas
2. Saturday ; Sunday
3. January ; New Year's Day
4. Easter
5. Tuesday

## 2 Nouns (2)

A. 1. flowers
2. owl
3. castle
4. kids

B. (Suggested drawings)

1.
mushrooms

2.
bears

3.
balloons

4.
stars

C. 1. sandwiches
2. glasses
3. dishes
4. boxes

D. 1. foxes
2. switches
3. addresses
4. bushes
5. benches

E. 1. beachs ; beaches
2. clownes ; clowns
3. brushs ; brushes
4. leges ; legs

## 3 Pronouns

A. He: F ; G
She: A ; H
It: B ; D
They: C ; E

B. 1. they          2. he
3. they          4. it
5. she           6. he
7. it            8. she

C. 1. They          2. She
3. It            4. They
5. He            6. It

D. 1. I            2. We
3. We           4. I
5. I            6. I
7. I            8. you

E. 1. We went to the beach.
2. It was a beautiful beach.
3. He built a sandcastle.
4. It was as tall as Paul.
5. She found two sand dollars.
6. They were light pink in colour.
7. Kate asked, "Can I keep the sand dollars?"

## 4 Articles

A.

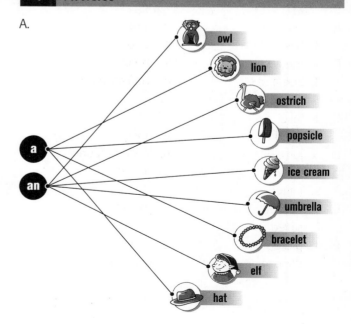

owl
lion
ostrich
popsicle
ice cream
umbrella
bracelet
elf
hat

a
an

B. 1. a penguin
3. an egg
5. a cake
7. a hippo
9. an apple

2. an elephant
4. an octopus
6. a bird
8. an owl
10. a top

C. 1. the CN Tower
3. the Great Lakes

2. the Parliament Buildings
4. the Canadian flag

D. 1. The ; the
3. The ; an
5. The ; the

2. The ; the
4. a

E. 1. The penguin lives in the South Pole.
2. The boy in the story is helpful.
3. You need to buy an orange and a watermelon.
4. The Parker family visited the CNE.

## 5 Verbs (1)

A. 1. C
3. E
5. A

2. D
4. B
6. F

B. 1. goes
3. works
5. give

2. collect
4. likes

C. 1. swim
3. runs

2. play
4. builds

D. 1. are
3. is

2. is
4. am

E. 1. is
3. is
5. is
7. am

2. am
4. are
6. are
8. is

## 6 Verbs (2)

A. 1. act
3. hits

2. cooks
4. collect

B. 1. the cat
3. Zoe and I
5. the players

2. the girls
4. the kangaroo

C. 1. take
3. need

2. tells
4. opens

D. 3. jumped
7. tied
9. rained

4. looked ; found
8. shared

E. 1. danced
3. saved

2. picked
4. learned

F. 1. picked
3. danced

2. saved
4. learned

## Progress Test 1

A. (Circle these common nouns.)
firefly ; light ; mom ; dad ; farm
mom ; light
Fireflies ; lights ; beetles ; dad
friends ; ladybug ; cricket ; cockroach ; mantis ; dog ; dog ;
problems
friends ; log ; grass
(Underline these proper nouns.)
Ray ; Farmer Sam
Ray
Ray ; Jane ; Kelly ; Ted ; Dave ; Jane ; Kelly ; Ted ; Dave ;
Kingsley ; Farmer Sam
Monday ; June

B. (Suggested answers)
Common Noun
1. mom
3. farm
Proper Noun
5. Farmer Sam
7. Monday

2. firefly
4. light

6. Kingsley
8. June

C. 1. dog
3. cockroaches
5. ladybugs

2. mantises
4. firefly

D. 1. we
3. we
5. I
7. we
9. It
11. They

2. He
4. You
6. you
8. you / we
10. She

E. 1. the ; the
3. the ; an
5. a ; the

2. a
4. a ; the ; the
6. The ; the ; the

F. 1. is
3. peeks
5. come
7. pulls
9. hears ; is ; need

2. am ; thinks
4. is
6. finds
8. stays

G. 1. Ray was the only one that Ted failed to find.
2. Ray suddenly remembered his light.
3. He and his friends walked back to the tree log.
4. They talked happily about the game on the way.
5. When they reached the log, they discovered that Ray's
light was gone.

## 7 Adjectives

A. 1. sad girl
3. beautiful butterfly
5. fast plane

2. cold drink
4. stormy weather
6. fat pig

ISBN: 978-1-897457-01-6

B. 1. long
   2. fierce
   3. slow
   4. bright
C. (Individual answers)
D. 1. a yellow mango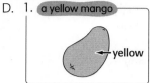
   2. two lollipops
   3. a blue kite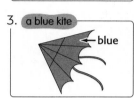
   4. four stars
   5. a brown teddy bear
   6. five apples
E. 1. an oval dish
   2. a square mirror
   3. a tiny bee
   4. a huge bear
   5. a round globe

## 8  Location Words

A. 1. beside
   2. under
   3. in
   4. above
   5. on
   6. behind
B. 1. on
   2. in
   3. behind
   4. above
   5. beside
   6. under
C. (Individual drawing and colouring)
D. (Suggested writing)
   1. There are two fairies in the basket.
   2. There is a butterfly on the sunflower.
   3. There are three flowers beside the basket.
   4. The apples are behind the fairies.
   5. A bee is flying above the basket.
   6. There is a snail under the sunflower.

## 9  Sentences

A. 1. ☹    2. ☺
   3. ☹    4. ☺
   5. ☹    6. ☺
   7. ☹    8. ☺
B. 1. D
   2. A
   3. E
   4. B
   5. C
C. 1. I like chewing gum.
   2. We buy gum in a candy shop.
   3. Bubble gum has many flavours.
D. 1. Grandpa and Grandma
   2. The school bus
   3. Monkeys
   4. Nina
   5. The duck
   6. Rome
   7. Summer
   8. Zeta and Alice
   9. The aliens
E. 1. C
   2. B
   3. A
   4. D
F. (Individual writing)

## 10  Types of Sentences

A. (Colour the boxes of 1, 2, 6, 8, and 9.)
B. 1. ✗    2. ✔    3. ✗
   4. ✔    5. ✗    6. ✗
   7. ✔    8. ✔    9. ✔
C. 1. S    2.      3.
   4.      5. S    6.
   7.      8. S    9. S
D. (Individual writing)
   1. Telling    2. Surprising
   3. Surprising    4. Asking

## 11  Punctuation and Capitalization

A. 1. .    2. !    3. .
   4. .    5. .    6. ?
   7. ?    8. !    9. !
B. 1. ? ; !    2. ✔    3. ! ; .    4. ✔
   5. ? ; .    6. . ; ?    7. ! ; ?    8. ✔
   9. . ; !    10. ✔

# Answers

C. 1. Aunt Stella
   3. Lake Ontario
   7. Shoppers Drug Mart
   8. Toronto Zoo
   9. Monday
D. 1. Tyra named her dog Casey.
   2. Thanksgiving Day is in October.
   3. Ian lives on Scottfield Crescent.
   4. How did Jason get the key?
   5. My sister was sick last Thursday.
   6. The Gardners went to Italy for a holiday.
   7. Roald Dahl wrote "Charlie and the Chocolate Factory".

## 12 Word Order in Sentences

A. 1. The robbers stole the car.
   2. Jamie put the cat in the basket.
   3. The children are sitting at the table.
   4. Sharon turned on the computer.
   5. My sister goes to Westside School.
B. (Individual writing)
   1.

   2.

   3.

C. 1. A bird is in the sky.
   2. There is a farmhouse on the farm.
   3. Smith is feeding the chicks.
   4. The boys have big baskets.
   5. Jerry has collected some potatoes.
D. 1. Sally ate an ice cream cone.
   2. They are skating at the rink.
   3. You need a key to open the chest.
   4. Dad bought a toy car for me.
   5. The puppy is sleeping on the couch.

## 13 Synonyms and Antonyms

A. 1. ☺    2. ☹    3. ☹
   4. ☺    5. ☺    6. ☺
   7. ☹    8. ☹    9. ☺
B. 1. glad         2. high
   3. breezy       4. hop
   5. dim
C. 1. The kids have fun at the party.
   2. Your room is really clean.
   3. The show starts at eight o'clock.
   4. This ice cream is so delicious!
D. 1.
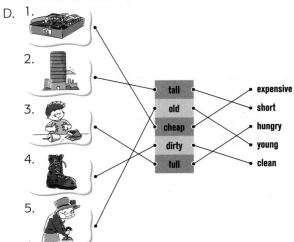

E.
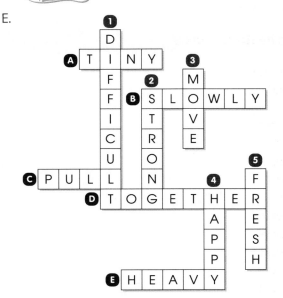

## Progress Test 2

A. (Circle these adjectives.)
   four ; good ; happy ; terrible ; lost
   missing ; old ; tall ; three ; wooden
   wise ; able
   red ; late ; asleep

ISBN: 978-1-897457-01-6

B. 1. on

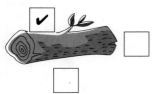

2. under

3. in

4. behind

5. beside

6. above

C. Ray and his friends wake Kingsley up. Kingsley asks them what happened. They tell him that Ray's light is lost. Kingsley sits there and closes his eyes. He doesn't speak for a long while. Then a big smile appears on his face. He opens his eyes. He seems to have found a solution to the problem. Ray looks eagerly at him.

D. 1. Do you know where my light is, Kingsley? ; A
2. Can you think of anyone that likes lights? ; A
3. Is it Molly the Moth? ; A
4. The five friends ask in unison. ; T
5. Where does Molly live? ; A
6. She lives in Farmer Sam's barn. ; T
7. Kingley, how clever you are! ; S

E. 1. The five friends get to the barn at once.
2. Ray's light is right there in the middle of Molly's table.
3. The light is giving out a warm glow.
4. The little friends are so happy to see Ray's light again.
5. Ray has never found his light so beautiful.

F. 1. asks
2. love
3. beautiful
4. come
5. glad
6. late
7. lose

ISBN: 978-1-897457-01-6

### 1  The Rainbow

A. 1. red     2. yellow
    3. blue     4. orange
    5. gold     6. purple

Challenge
    gold ; nickel

B. 1. today     2. yellow
    3. red     4. Orange
    5. gold     6. blue

C. 1. pot     2. orange
    3. luck     4. rainbow
    5. school     6. end

D. 1. blue     2. end
    3. pot     4. school
    5. that     6. red

E.

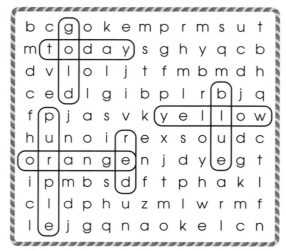

F. 1. purple     2. school
    3. orange     4. luck
    5. yellow     6. blue
    7. people     8. gold

### 2  My Farm Visit

A. 1. dad     2. farm
    3. city     4. barn
    5. sister

B.

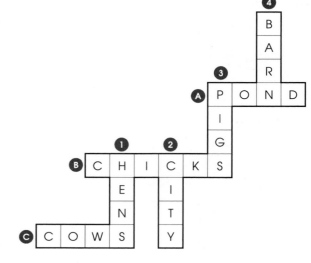

C. (Circle 1, 2, 3, 4, 5, 8, 9, and 10.)
    1. chick     2. cheese
    3. duck     4. pond
    5. pig     6. city
    7. toys     8. barn
    9. rooster     10. tractor

D.

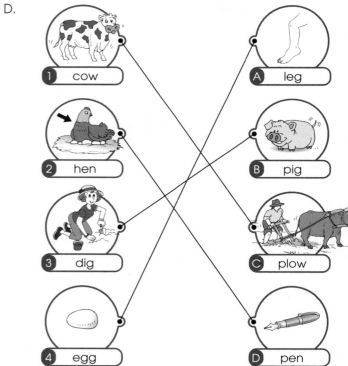

### 3  The Visit

A. 1. visit     2. aunt
    3. uncle     4. airplane
    5. cousins     6. rides
    7. wave     8. went

ISBN: 978-1-897457-01-6

B. 1. cat      2. pool
   3. boat      4. tree
   5. week      6. aunt
   7. uncle      8. cousins
   9. airplane      10. tower
   11. paddle      12. year

C. 1. fire      2. tent
   3. pool      4. boat
   5. duck      6. nest
   7. net      8. boot
   9. bug      10. lake

D. (Colour these pictures.)

1. The man drove the car.

2. The cat climbed the tree.

3. The boy rode a bike.

4. The dog ate the bone.

## 4   The New Pet

A. 1. Sunday      2. Monday
   3. Tuesday      4. Wednesday
   5. Thursday      6. Friday
   7. Saturday

B. (Colour 2, 3, 5, 9, and 10.)
   1. B      2. E
   3. F      4. H
   5. A      6. D

   7. L      8. K
   9. J      10. I
   11. C      12. G

C. 1. dogs      2. animal
   3. cats      4. tabby
   5. brown      6. place
   7. orange      8. kinds
   9. male

D.

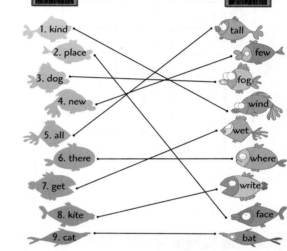

## 5   The Tree-House

A. 1. friends      2. tree-house
   3. First      4. house
   5. look      6. hammer
   7. saw      8. nails
   9. wood      10. friends
   11. time      12. sun
   13. moon      14. tree-house

B.

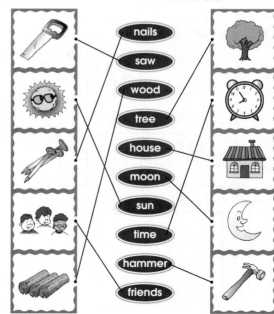

C. 1. nails      2. hammer
   3. saw       4. wood
   5. hard     6. sun
   7. moon    8. friends
   9. look    10. need
  11. work   12. tools
  13. time   14. busy
  15. finished

D.

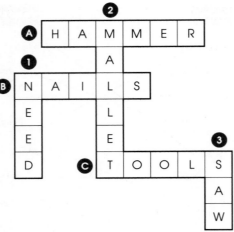

## 6   At the Beach

A. 1. Sunday   2. beach
   3. friends   4. lunch
   5. sand    6. ocean
B. 1. beach   2. ball
   3. swim    4. sun
   5. lunch   6. sky
   7. friends  8. sea
   9. sand
C. (Individual writing)
Challenge
   (Individual writing)
D.

## 7   Bill and Bob

A.   Bill and Bob are (twins). This means that they were born on the same (day), about the same (time) from the same mom. Today is their (birthday). They are both (six) (years) old. They are (brothers).

  Bill and Bob like some of the same things. They like to (swim) and (skate). They also like different things. Bob likes to (draw) and Bill likes to (play) video games.

  Best of all, Bill and Bob are good (friends) who like each other.

B. 1. C     2. I
   3. G     4. J
   5. A     6. D
   7. L     8. E
   9. K    10. F
  11. B    12. H
C. 1. twins   2. time
   3. six    4. swim
   5. skate   6. brothers
   7. draw   8. play
D.

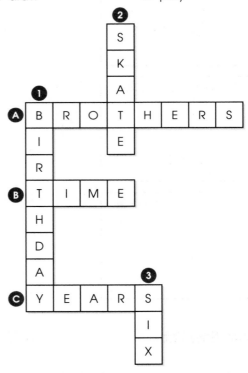

## Progress Test 1

A. 1. ride – pride
   2. bite – kite
   3. try – sky
   4. run – fun

5. bone – stone
6. dime – time
7. mile – smile
8. kit – bit
9. pot – lot
10. top – mop
11. bale – tale
12. hug – bug

B. 1. gold      2. airplane
    3. blue      4. cow
    5. orange      6. farm
    7. boat      8. end
    9. ladybug      10. tent

C. 1. yellow      2. today
    3. blue      4. school
    5. farm      6. barn
    7. sister      8. cows
    9. boats      10. went
    11. wave      12. visit

D. 1. L      2. H
    3. F      4. C
    5. G      6. I
    7. A      8. E
    9. J      10. K
    11. D      12. B

E. 1. The bone chewed the dog. ✗
    2. The fish ate the whale. ✗
    3. The nut ate the squirrel. ✗
    4. The sky fell from the rain. ✗
    5. The leaf crawled on the bug. ✗

F. 1. N      2. J
    3. B      4. C
    5. I      6. K
    7. E      8. D
    9. H      10. O
    11. G      12. A
    13. L      14. F
    15. M

## 8   A Picture Story

A. (Individual writing)
B. 1. There were lots of trees.
    2. The family went camping.
    3. They had to sleep in a tent.
    4. Do people like peanut butter sandwiches?
    5. Bears do too!
    6. The bears ate the food.
    7. Do bears like picnics?

C. trees ; chair ; tent ; pegs ; flap ; pot ; swim ; picnic ; fire ; table

D. 1. tent      2. camp
    3. tree      4. picnic
    5. pegs      6. food
    7. fire      8. flap

E. 1. My dad and I like to hike.  We have a favourite trail. ~~The treats were good.~~
    2. My family went on a picnic. ~~The car was dirty.~~  We had peanut butter sandwiches.
    3. Mom and I like to swim. ~~There were lots of caves.~~  We swim in the lake.
    4. Bears like honey.  They climb trees to get it. ~~My favourite food is pizza.~~

## 9   Swimming Fun

A. 1. swimsuit      2. swim
    3. swimming pool      4. friends
    5. house      6. girls
    7. ball

B. (Suggested answers)
    1. ball ; call ; fall ; hall ; mall ; tall
    2. dim ; him ; Jim ; Kim ; rim ; Tim
    3. bin ; fin ; kin ; pin ; tin ; win
    4. cool ; fool ; pool ; tool
    5. dot ; got ; hot ; lot
    6. bad ; dad ; lad ; sad

C. (Individual writing)
D.

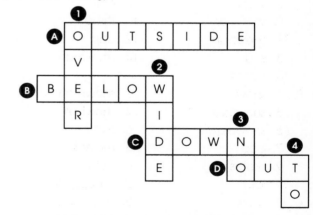

## 10   The Yellow Duck

A. 1. back      2. duck
    3. duck      4. pecked
    5. chick      6. chick
    7. duck      8. quack
    9. duck      10. chick
    11. duck      12. pecked
    13. licked

B.

Crossword:
- A: JACKET
- B: CLOCK
- C: POCKETS
- 1 (down): LUCKY
- 2 (down): TICKE (T-I-C-K-E...)
- 3 (down): KICK

C. (Suggested answers)
1. hack ; lack ; pack ; rack ; sack ; tack
2. deck ; peck
3. lick ; nick ; pick ; sick ; tick ; wick
4. cock ; hock ; mock ; rock ; sock
5. buck ; luck ; puck ; suck ; tuck

D. 
1. clock
2. duck
3. wick
4. luck
5. kick
6. pocket

## 11  A Rebus Story

A. 
1. Snowman
2. snowman
3. snow
4. ball
5. two
6. balls
7. snow
8. one
9. snowball
10. three
11. snowballs
12. cap
13. scarf
14. snowman
15. carrot

B. 
1. snow
2. snowman
3. snowflake
4. snowball
5. snowplow
6. scarf
7. cap
8. mittens
9. skates
10. cold
11. ice
12. toboggan

C. 
1. snow
2. snowman
3. cap ; mittens
4. toboggan
5. skates
6. scarf
7. cold
8. snowball

D. 
1. G
2. E
3. H
4. F
5. B
6. D
7. A
8. C

## 12  The Doctor's Tools

A. 
1. Doctors have "tools" that they use.
2. Daniel went for his check-up.
3. The nurse took his temperature with a thermometer.
4. Dr. Conn used a "reflex hammer" on his knees.

B. 
1. doctor
2. tools
3. hammer
4. thermometer
5. nurse
6. funny
7. temperature
8. fun

C. (Individual writing)

D.

1. thermometer
2. screwdriver
3. reflex hammer
4. ruler
5. saw
6. rake
7. shovel

A. tool used to draw lines and measure length
B. cutting tool
C. tool used to measure body temperature
D. tool used to gather leaves
E. tool used for turning screws
F. tool used to lift snow or soil
G. tool used by a doctor to check reflexes

## 13  Buzzing Bees

A. 
1. busy
2. insects
3. worker
4. queen
5. buzz
6. flowers
7. plants
8. suck
9. nectar
10. carry
11. food
12. sacs
13. hive
14. honey
15. sweet
16. good

B. 
1. B
2. E
3. A
4. D
5. H
6. G
7. C
8. F

C. 
1. buzz
2. sacs
3. queen bee
4. flowers
5. nectar
6. hive
7. bee
8. honey

ISBN: 978-1-897457-01-6

D.

| b | e | a | s | n | m | e | s | c | u | j | o | r | i | d | k | h | q | f |
|---|---|---|---|---|---|---|---|---|---|---|---|---|---|---|---|---|---|---|
| f | d | q | t | i | e | y | n | w | l | p | b | n | v | a | t | m | w | p |
| s | a | c | s | a | v | h | i | v | e | t | m | w | g | c | d | x | b | j |
| b | o | j | p | k | s | d | y | h | h | f | e | q | u | e | e | n | s | v |
| m | b | c | h | q | q | r | p | k | o | i | y | a | h | u | s | p | t | i |
| i | s | r | b | e | e | s | e | l | b | r | t | s | e | c | q | j | p | g |
| n | d | m | v | c | w | v | i | t | c | b | u | z | z | r | k | z | l | u |
| s | l | a | j | a | g | a | f | w | l | t | d | v | u | t | a | w | a | l |
| e | e | u | s | f | d | n | m | s | h | c | m | p | h | d | y | m | n | f |
| c | n | i | n | e | c | t | a | r | e | u | p | y | g | d | p | m | t | s |
| t | g | k | t | p | w | j | l | n | x | j | h | o | n | e | y | r | s | m |
| k | v | q | c | x | b | k | m | d | v | z | c | p | l | z | i | t | a | q |
| c | b | l | o | r | l | i | x | u | o | n | a | o | z | b | k | g | o | x |
| i | n | h | g | j | x | s | w | e | e | t | z | w | h | u | a | m | j | d |
| f | l | o | w | e | r | s | v | t | c | p | b | x | r | e | l | c | s | h |
| e | k | b | n | m | o | c | h | k | d | q | i | f | w | o | r | k | e | r |

## 14　The Bus Ride

A. 1. flowers　　　2. change
　　3. store　　　　4. money
　　5. coins　　　　6. driver
B. 1. flowers　　　2. driver
　　3. bell　　　　4. coins
　　5. store　　　　6. Monday
　　7. money　　　8. bus
C. 1. coin　　　　2. bell
　　3. money　　　4. store
　　5. Monday　　6. change
　　7. flowers
D. 1. We like to take bus rides.
　　2. The bus driver wears a hat.
　　3. We rang the bell to stop the bus.
　　4. We had lots of fun!
　　5. Do you ride the bus?
　　6. I ride on a school bus.

## 15　My Favourite Monster

A. Number : two ; three ; four ; five
　　Body parts : eyes ; fur ; fingers ; hand ; toes ; foot ; teeth ;
　　　　　　　　mouth
B. (Individual drawings)
C. 1. favourite　　2. scary
　　3. fingers　　　4. closet
　　5. teeth　　　　6. monster
　　7. friendly
D. 1. monster　　　2. lives
　　3. closet　　　　4. scary
　　5. friendly　　　6. two
　　7. big　　　　　8. green
　　9. pink　　　　10. fur

11. three　　　　12. fingers
13. four　　　　　14. five
15. toes　　　　　16. foot
17. teeth　　　　18. bed
19. go　　　　　　20. night

### Progress Test 2

A. (Individual writing)
B. (Suggested answers)
　　1. family　　　　2. rabbit
　　3. store　　　　4. saleslady
　　5. store　　　　6. rabbits
　　7. dogs　　　　8. cats
　　9. turtles　　　10. birds
　　11. store　　　12. love
　　13. dog　　　　14. mom
　　15. dogs　　　16. walk
C.

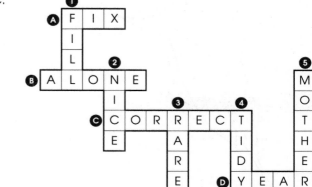

D. 1. B　　　　　2. E
　　3. A　　　　　4. F
　　5. D　　　　　6. I
　　7. G　　　　　8. J
　　9. C　　　　　10. H
E. 1. swim　　　　2. kick
　　3. snow　　　　4. money
　　5. trees　　　　6. clock
　　7. lucky　　　　8. scarf
　　9. store　　　10. picnic
　　11. jacket　　12. skates
　　13. driver
F. 1. We like to skate in winter.
　　2. Ron is a bus driver.
　　3. Kathy loves to read books.
　　4. Mandy swims in the pool at her house.
　　5. Do you like to cook?
　　6. My new coat is blue.

1.
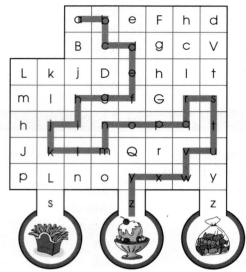

2.
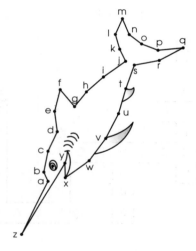

3.

4. (Individual drawing)

5.

We rarely see other polar bears on this bare land of snow.

We do not find any penguins here either.

6.

| e | k | r | q | d | c | j | b | o | m | q | h |
|---|---|---|---|---|---|---|---|---|---|---|---|
| j | a | n | f | t | v | n | s | d | o | g | i |
| u | c | a | t | y | g | w | f | r | u | d | l |
| p | h | l | m | u | m | a | v | p | s | e | p |
| s | x | g | f | o | z | i | t | s | e | c | a |
| f | c | l | i | b | l | h | o | g | k | j | r |
| v | d | i | s | e | x | r | r | d | n | t | r |
| i | o | z | h | a | j | a | t | s | z | b | o |
| l | w | a | x | m | u | b | o | y | f | q | t |
| b | i | r | d | y | e | b | i | p | w | h | r |
| m | z | d | k | r | b | i | s | t | o | a | m |
| g | c | h | a | m | s | t | e | r | d | k | i |

7.
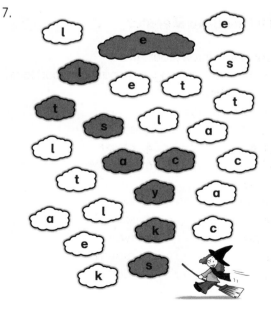

ISBN: 978-1-897457-01-6

8.
- ■ purple
- ☐ blue
- ■ green
- ■ black
- ☐ white

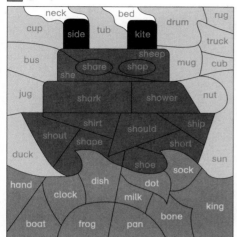

9.
1. dress
2. hat
3. mug
4. tent
5. doll
6. bird
7. bell

10.

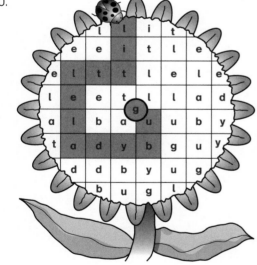

11.

12. 1. carrot
2. pear
3. mushroom
4. mango
5. eggplant
6. pineapple
7. tomato
8. watermelon

13.

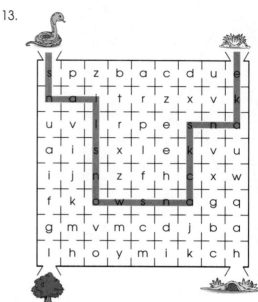

14. candle → skull → web → rope → spider → bat → coffin → ghost

15.

| n | q | d | b | j | g | y | k | m | d | l | o |
|---|---|---|---|---|---|---|---|---|---|---|---|
| p | t | c | i | n | x | r | w | b | u | g | s |
| l | r | o | r | p | s | b | u | a | c | p | g |
| s | e | t | d | x | k | m | f | z | k | w | s |
| g | e | e | s | e | i | z | l | e | s | s | w |
| k | s | r | m | w | d | p | o | n | d | v | i |
| t | d | b | i | l | s | b | w | h | p | x | n |
| e | q | b | e | n | c | h | e | s | c | m | g |
| h | l | n | s | q | u | i | r | r | e | l | s |
| b | s | l | i | d | e | g | s | f | a | k | r |

16.

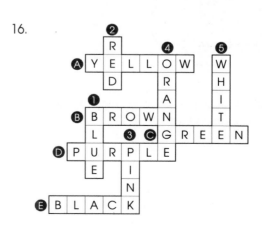

ISBN: 978-1-897457-01-6

17.

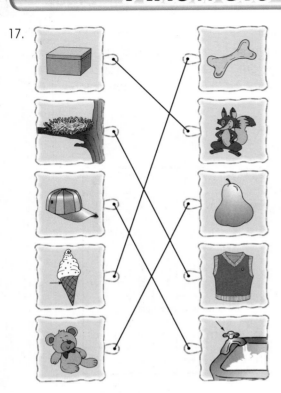

20. (Individual drawing of the ring)
1. ring
2. king
3. wing
4. wind
5. wand
6. sand
7. hand

18.

| | body | icy |
| easy | tent | |
| see | dog | gold |
| able | begin | enjoy |
| run | wash | sing |
| ever | clock | hero |
| area | over | cup |
| windy | boxes | pen |
| lion | lake | argue |
| after | bed | cosy |
| draw | very | |
| come | lazy | horse |
| hide | ring | |
| basin | dress | user |
| about | | |
| level | pizza | |

19. snail → duck → bell → moon → swing → candy
→ smile → acorn → leaf